D1595959

THE SHADOW OF THE WHITE ROSE

THE SHADOW OF THE WHITE ROSE

Edward Courtenay
Earl of Devon
1526-1556

James D. Taylor, Jr.

Algora Publishing
New York

ISBN: 0-87586-473-2 (trade soft)
ISBN: 0-87586-474-0 (hard cover)
ISBN: 0-87586-475-9 (ebook)

Library of Congress Cataloging-in-Publication Data —

Taylor, James D., 1958-

    The shadow of the White Rose: Edward Courtenay, Earl of Devon,
1526-1556 / James D. Taylor, Jr.

        p. cm.

Includes bibliographical references and index.

ISBN 0-87586-473-2 (trade paper: alk. paper) — ISBN 0-87586-474-0
(hard cover: alk. paper) — ISBN 0-87586-475-9 (ebook) 1. Devon,
Edward Courtenay, Earl of, 1526-1556. 2. Great Britain—History—
Mary I, 1553-1558—Biography. 3. Great Britain—History—Edward VI,
1547-1553—Biography. 4. Great Britain—Politics and government—
1485-1603. 5. Nobility—England—Biography. I. Title.

DA347.1.D48T39 2006

942.05'4092—dc22

                        2006005330

Equo ne credite, Teucri,
Quidquid est, timeo Danaos et dona ferentes.

Do not trust the horse, Trojans.
Whatever it is, I fear the Greeks even when they bring gifts.
(Virgil, 70-19 BC, Aeneid)

ACKNOWLEDGEMENTS

A very warm thank you to Lady Katherine Watney, Chairman of the Courtenay Society, Powderham Castle, Kenton, Exeter, Devon, England.

Special thanks to the University of Michigan at Ann Arbor, Wayne State University, Michigan State University, and the British Library, whose vast holdings, resources, and patient staff have made this work possible.

I am also grateful to the staff at Purdue University; Pitts Theology Library at Emory University; the Bodleian Library and Ashmolean Library at Oxford University; the William Andrew Clark Memorial Library at the University of California; the Folger Shakespeare Library; the Special Collections Department at the Alderman Memorial Library at the University of Virginia; and Charlene Berry at Madonna University for her spiritual support throughout this project.

Last but not least is Sarah, whose patience should not go unmentioned on this project.

Thank you all.

TABLE OF CONTENTS

Edward's Family Ancestral Tree

TABLE 1

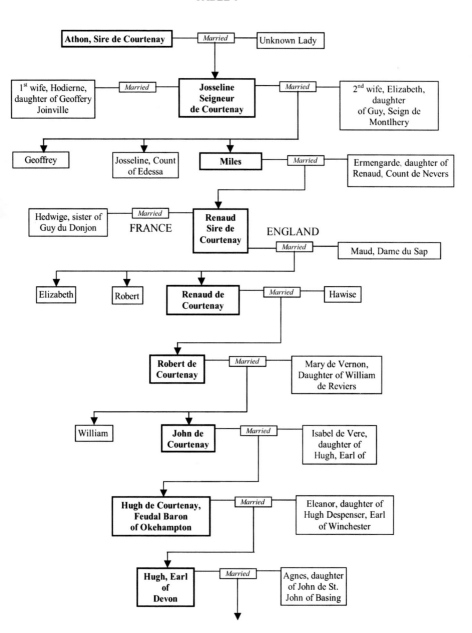

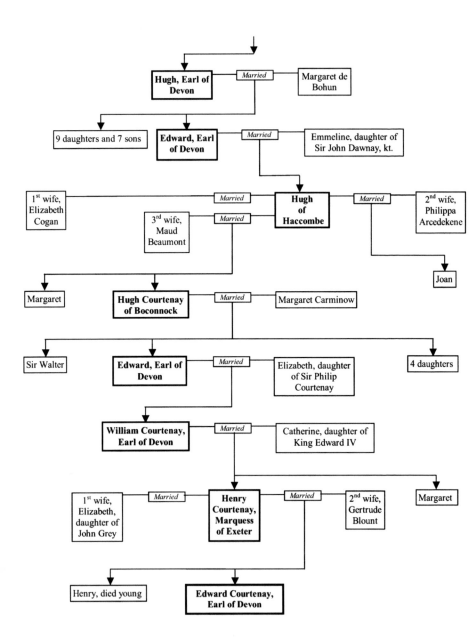

Edward's Royal Ancestral Tree

TABLE 2

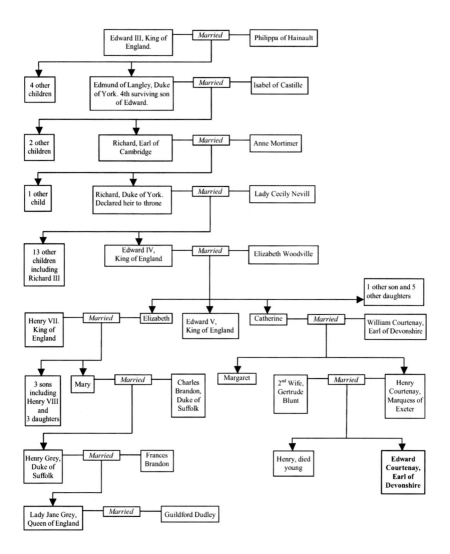

INTRODUCTION

Edward Courtenay, the Earl of Devon, walked a fine line that separated treason and loyalty to the crown, just as several of his ancestors had done.

It became fairly clear to me, during this five-year project of reviewing the surviving correspondence to and from Courtenay and other documentation from the period, that what survives for the most part was allowed to survive. After Courtenay's death, a report from the Council of Ten in Venice indicated that a large cache of his writings existed.[1] The Council of Ten in Venice hired a carpenter to open the sealed box containing Courtenay's literary remains and swore him to secrecy. After they reviewed the contents, they removed a certain quantity, replaced the remainder the way they were first discovered, and resealed the box. Many letters were never seen again.

It is safe to speculate that the letters the Council removed contained references to such important political or personal information that someone was willing to commit a crime to prevent their contents from ever being read. Certainly, the French would have had the greatest interest in those letters.

---

1. Mentioned in several letters from *The Calendar of State Papers and Manuscripts relating to English Affairs, Venice* Vol. VI 1556-1557 edited by Rawdon Brown.

Perhaps the most frustrating to me was the constant evidence of gaps in documents in the correspondence from the last three months of his life, where a letter should exist but does not. Intriguing are several instances when Courtenay's name was purposely omitted from the translation or decipherment of correspondence that was most likely related to the affairs of King Henry II of France and his ambassadors in England.

Courtenay is often absent from biographies on subjects from the period. When he is mentioned, he is described as a "bumbling buffoon," ignorant, dull witted, or rash. He was actually quite the contrary, as I hope the material in this book will demonstrate.

Courtenay spent over half of his life imprisoned in the Tower of London for crimes that his father had committed during the reign of King Henry VIII. Mary Tudor finally released him when she seized the throne from Jane Grey after only a nine-day reign, and Courtenay was soon regarded as a worthy husband for Mary. After repeatedly rejecting all advances of marriage and showing no interest in the prospect of being king, it was decided that he should marry Elizabeth, who was next in the order of succession to the crown, but Courtenay was not interested in that prospect, either.

Mary then announced that her choice for a husband was Prince Philip of Spain. This was not a popular choice with many in the realm and led to the Wyatt rebellion, in which Mary was almost removed from the throne by force (Courtenay and Elizabeth were to reign in her place).

Courtenay was again imprisoned, but this time only on suspicion, as any evidence that could have been used against him had been altered or destroyed. Released about a year later, he was sent out of England, whereupon he traveled through France, Belgium, and Germany, and finally arrived in Italy, where his activities will most likely remain enshrouded in the shadow of the White Rose.

CHAPTER 1. EDWARD COURTENAY'S ANCESTRY

The information contained in this chapter regarding Edward Courtenay's ancestry is based on information from two sources: *A Genealogical History of the Noble and Illustrious Family of Courtenay*, by E. Cleaveland, London, 1735, and *Burke's Genealogical and Heraldic History of the Peerage Baronetage and Knightage*, by Bernard Burke, London 1967. The Courtenay family has numerous branches, but this chapter will only cover those who are direct ancestors of Edward Courtenay.

Edward Courtenay, the Earl of Devon, belonged to a distinguished family that took its name from the town of Courtenay, located on a hill near the banks of the River Clairy about 50 miles south of Paris, France.

The Courtenay family branch that this book is concerned with begins with Athon, the son of a French governor who rendered himself famous through his accomplishments and fortified the castle of Courtenay. From this the family took its name, at about the time surnames were first being used in France, during the reign of King Robert of France and just before the Norman conquest of AD 1066. History has recorded very little about the woman whom Athon married, other than the fact that she was of noble blood and that she died in about the year AD 1040. This woman gave him a son, Josseline Sire de Courtenay, who had three children through his second marriage, to Elizabeth, daughter of Guy de Montlhery. It is through these three children that each of the three noble branches originate.

The first of these branches seated itself in the east part of France and flourished there for some time under the name of the Count of Edessa; the second branch, which descended from Peter the youngest son of Louis de Gros, King of France, who boasted his rank among the princes of the blood line next to the House of Bourbon, stayed in France. Finally, the third branch, from the time of Henry II to Mary Tudor's days, lived in England under the titles of Baron, Earl, and Marques, and had several times married into the Royal Family.

This chapter will cover this third branch in some detail, all the way up to the time of Edward Courtenay, the subject of this biography. The line begins with Miles Sire de Courtenay who was instrumental as founder of the Cistercian Abbey of Fontaine-Jean. In about 1127 he married Ermengarde, daughter of Renaud, Count de Nevers, and she gave birth to three children. It is through one of these three children, Renaud Sire de Courtenay, that the family branch continues.

RENAUD SIRE DE COURTENAY

Renaud Sire de Courtenay was born and raised in France. Renaud later accompanied King Louis VII of France on the Second Crusade in 1147, which was led by the Holy Roman Emperor Conrad III, whose army set out first, and by King Louis VII of France. Both armies passed through the Balkans and pillaged the territory of the Byzantine Emperor Manuel I, who provided them with transportation to Asia Minor in order to be rid of them. The Crusade failed, and King Louis returned to France in 1149.

In 1152, King Louis suspected that his queen, Eleanor of Aquitanie, was unfaithful and had the marriage annulled. Eleanor quickly departed for England where she and King Henry II of England married in May 1152. History suggests that during a major disagreement with King Louis VII of France, Renaud Courtenay sided with Queen Eleanor and, fearing retribution, joined her when she returned to England in 1154. It is through Renaud that the Courtenay family began its long history in England.

Although the marriage of Eleanor and Henry has been described as a happy relationship that lasted for many years, it has also been suggested that Eleanor poisoned Henry's later love, Rosamund Clifford. Henry II was the first of the Plantagenets on the throne and he possessed many good qualities such as being brave, prudent, and generous. With a strong and stocky frame, his lust and ambitions were insatiable and his temper was typical of the Plantagenet line, which could at times become exceedingly violent.

Renaud Sire de Courtenay's first marriage was to Hedwige, sister of Guy du Donjon while he was still in France. It is not clear what happened between Renaud de Courtenay and his first wife, but the conditions in which Renaud left his homeland may have included her death. While in England, he married Maud Dame du Sap, daughter of Robert fitz Roy (natural son of King Henry I), and by her had a son, Renaud.

RENAUD DE COURTENAY

History suggests that Renaud de Courtenay gained some of his titles (sheriff of Devon and Castellan of Exeter) through his second marriage, to Hawise, which was arranged by King Henry II in appreciation for his introduction to Eleanor. Renaud was certainly well respected and trusted by the English King as numerous accounts indicate that Renaud accompanied the King wherever he went, including several wars and campaigns; because of his contributions, many regarded him as a noble and valiant soldier. Renaud de Courtenay's name appears on several documents as a witness to the many deeds and charters that King Henry made, which were mainly in the form of grants to churches. He was given a special license by the Pope to have a free chapel at Okehampton in Devon. Renaud himself contributed both money and gifts, and having received the blessing of "both God and Man," monks blessed him when he died during the sixth year of King Richard's reign.

Renaud was married in about 1178 to Hawise, Lady of Okehampton, daughter, and co-heiress of Maud d'Avranches. By his marriage to Hawise, he had a son, Robert who would succeed his father, carrying with him all his titles and estates.

ROBERT DE COURTENAY

History suggests that Robert de Courtenay paid off numerous debts in the beginning years of the reign of King John and besides paying with money, he also gave the King two great horses. To help Robert with some of his debts, the King agreed that Courtenay would serve his needs with twenty men-at-arms for a period of one full year. It has been suggested that the King made Robert de Courtenay the governor of Burges and issued a letter to the Constable introducing Courtenay and welcoming him to the castle. The King also sent a letter to the Castle of Bristol announcing that Robert de Courtenay and Walter de Verdum would occupy the castle with a garrison of soldiers for as long as the King desired it.

Very soon after, several gentlemen dissented against the King, who quickly commissioned Robert de Courtenay to lead the forces of William Brevere into the city of Exeter. Further orders were issued for the citizens of Exeter to assist Courtenay if his forces were inadequate in defending the city. The King later rewarded Courtenay for these actions and other services.

In the first year of the reign of Henry III, the King ordered Henry, son of Reginald, Earl of Cornwall, to turn the Castle of Exeter over to Robert de Courtenay, who maintained it for sixteen years before turning it over to Peter de Rival, a favorite of the King at the time. Robert de Courtenay did not fall out of favor with the King in the least and to show his appreciation to Courtenay for his many years of faithful service, the King gave him custody of the Castle of Plympton. The King had seized possession of the castle from William, Earl of Devon, a few years earlier. After this, Robert de Courtenay was no longer the Viscount of Devon but the Feudal Baron of Okehampton. Robert de Courtenay was also appointed the sheriff of Devon and Castellan of Exeter, and several prisoners where committed to his custody. In 1215, King John committed him all the coinage of tin in the counties of Devon and Cornwall.

The monks at Ford had many commendable things to say about Robert de Courtenay including his kindness towards them and consideration for their welfare; he often called them his fathers and patrons. History suggests that Courtenay gave some of his lands in the parish of Wolburough to the Abbey of Torre.

Robert de Courtenay, Feudal Baron of Okehampton, married Mary de Vernon (widow of Pierre de Peaux), youngest daughter of William de Reviers, fifth Earl of Devon and Lord of the Isle of Wight, and by her had a son, John, who would succeed his father with all his estates and titles.

JOHN DE COURTENAY

John de Courtenay Feudal Baron of Okehampton was most likely born either at the end of the reign of King John or during the beginning of the reign of Henry III. King John was given the nickname of "Lackland" by his father because of the lack of provisions that his father could offer him. King John is often remembered for being cruel and lacking honor, conscience, or religion, and these negative traits dominate most historical accounts. King John is best remembered for his issuance of the "Great Charter," the Magna Carta, which he signed at Runnymede, an island in the Thames River, in the year 1215. The clauses of the Magna Carta defined and limited the feudal rights of the king and protected the rights of the Church.

Upon the death of King John, his successor King Henry III was the first royal minor (aged about nine) to succeed to the throne in English history. Henry's reign, though lasting about 50 years, does not contain anything that would set it apart from other reigns. Often regarded as loving money, he squandered it idly. He participated in no noteworthy campaigns that would label him with valor, but he did contribute to culture and religion through the building and rebuilding of superb churches, which included the rebuilding the Confessor's Abbey at Westminster. King Henry III was regarded as the premier zookeeper of Western Europe as he kept the first elephant, bear, camel, lion, and three leopards in England.

History has indicated that John de Courtenay, son of Robert had to pay a large sum of money in relief of the debts that his father left after his death. Upon payment of these debts, John was restored to all of his honors and was also regarded as the Feudal Baron of Okehampton, though not by creation.

John de Courtenay accompanied Henry III on several campaigns including one into Gasteoign, Wales, and he later led a campaign in Bristol where he was instrumental in suppressing a hostile uprising of the Welsh. King Henry granted permission for John to hunt on his lands in Devonshire, Somersetshire, Dorset, Berkshire, and Buckinghamshire and he was made the Constable of the Castle of Totnes in Devon. Unfortunately, John was unable to obtain the castle in Exeter in the county of Devon that had been taken from his father by King Henry III.

John de Courtenay had the same reverence for the monks at Ford as did his predecessors and a story has survived that was passed down from their register in which John de Courtenay, while returning to England by sea, met a violent storm. When the crew panicked, Courtenay brought them to their senses through prayer and reassuring talk. The ship reached its port safely.

John Courtenay married Isabel, daughter of Hugh de Vere, fourth Earl of Oxford, and Lord High Chamberlain of England. Isabel gave birth to a son Hugh during the reign of Henry III.

HUGH DE COURTENAY

Hugh Courtenay was about twenty-three years old when his father died. He later accompanied King Edward I on an expedition into West Wales in 1282. Edward I was a colorful monarch who also possessed the Plantagenet temper. He has been described as being very tall with legs that were too long, which earned him the nickname of "Long Shanks." During the first years of his reign, he was regarded as being reckless and disloyal in his judgments, but he learned from these mistakes and became an excellent king who participated in numerous campaigns that would reinforce that image. Many benefited from what has been described as his "curative touch," including about a thousand Scots. Later in his reign, King Edward addressed a problem that a growing population must often deal with, pollution. One solution was to stop using sea-coal and use wood and regular coal for fires, and thus a great deal of soot was eliminated.

King Edward regarded Hugh as being well exercised in military affairs, and he granted Hugh a letter of protection while he was in the King's service with Roger de Bigod, Earl of Norfolk and Marshal of England, on a campaign into Wales. After several campaigns, Wales finally surrendered to King Edward and to celebrate Edward held a "round table" with knightly tournaments and dancing. In the same year, an unknown person murdered Walter Lieblade, the First Chanter of the Church of Exeter, possibly with the intent to rob him. The King, who also visited the church from time to time, drew up a contract to construct walls and gates around the church. Hugh de Courtenay witnessed the signing of the contract.

History suggests that the following year Hugh de Courtenay had a quarrel with the monks of Ford. Though the reason for the quarrel is unclear, several past generations of Courtenay's had granted the monks' requests and perhaps Hugh did not. Hugh even went so far as to take cattle and oxen from the monks and this led to a lawsuit filed by the monks that was later resolved, though rather bitterly. Shortly after that resolution, Hugh was accompanied by several men and set out to seek restitution from the monks, but members of the abbey prevented them from doing so and Hugh was unable to take any of their cattle. While Hugh was returning to his residence in

Colecomb, he took a bull, twelve cows, and four oxen, which permanently damaged relations between the Courtenay family and the monks and would not be resolved in Hugh's lifetime.

Hugh married Eleanor; daughter of Hugh Despencser Earl of Winchester and Justiciar of England and by her had a son Hugh, who would succeed his father in his honors and estates.

HUGH COURTENAY, EARL OF DEVON

Hugh Courtenay accompanied King Edward I on numerous campaigns into Scotland. With the death of King Alexander III of Scotland, Edward supported John Balliol for the throne instead of Robert Bruce and Edward's aggressiveness in the matter led to a war that lasted beyond the death of King Edward I. Speculation exists as to why King Edward I removed the "Stone of Destiny" on which the Scottish kings received their equivalent of a coronation and transported it to London, where the English King placed it on display for everyone to see as a sign that the kingdom of Scotland had been conquered. Hugh Courtenay also accompanied the King on a campaign into Wales. To show his appreciation to all those gallant men who supported him during those campaigns, the King held a ceremony at Westminster to pay them tribute; guests included Hugh Courtenay.

During the last year of his reign, King Edward I held a session of Parliament and Hugh was summoned to participate as Lord Courtenay, 1299-1334, an honor that a baron would not have had without the king's permission.

In the first year of the reign of King Edward II, Walter Stapleton was assigned the position of Bishop of Exeter. He was a gentleman of good quality and Hugh Courtenay, who believed that he was the steward and governor of the feast, led the bishop to the ceremony. After the ceremonies and feast were over, Hugh

Courtenay and the bishop had a dispute regarding the duties and rights of the position of steward. As a result of this dispute, eight conditions were drawn up which resolved the issue to the satisfaction of both individuals. Perhaps because of the dispute or as the result of its resolution, it has been stated that Hugh Courtenay received higher wages than the Earl of Gloucester, who had previously held the position, and this caused certain animosities between them.

In response to the possibility of war, Hugh Courtenay was given command over a large garrison of men and arms that were stationed in Newcastle to prevent any advancement by the Scots. Robert the Bruce and King Edward's forces did finally meet around the Bannock stream with the Scots forming a wedge of infantrymen armed with spears that inflicted many English casualties and secured a defeat over the English. King Edward was quickly swept away to safety and his forces retreated. Robert the Bruce demanded the return of the "Stone of Destiny" as part of the truce, but Edward rejected Bruce's demand — as he did all of his demands.

The following year saw the end for King Edward II, as his Queen Isabella departed England to the court of her brother, Charles IV of Spain. There she began to plot Edward's downfall in spite of his numerous requests for her to return to England. News of her intentions leaked out and the following year Isabella returned to England.

A session of Parliament concluded the same year with a decision that the King should resign his crown; and messengers consisting of two bishops, two earls, two abbots and two barons, Roger Gray and Hugh Courtenay, were sent to the King informing him of Parliament's decision. King Edward II was soon captured and suffered a violent death by the design of Isabella. There is a story that has survived that Isabella had Edward's heart removed and placed in a "guilt box" that was later buried with her.

Shortly after Edward III ascended the throne, Hugh Courtenay was assigned by Parliament to meet with the King of France and later Hugh was assigned to keep the peace in the county of Devon. Hugh Courtenay was the first name on the list with the first commission of the peace awarded in that county.

On 22 February 1335, Hugh was declared by letters patent to the title of Earl of Devon and enjoyed all the pomp that came with it. Though King Edward III was only about fifteen when he ascended the throne, he had learned from his father's mistakes and acquired a great deal of knowledge in military affairs. Edward III is perhaps best remembered for the Hundred Years War with France.

In the same year that war broke out, Hugh, Earl of Devon was given a commission to command the forces required to protect the seas in Devon and Cornwall. He died three years later, and soon after his death disputes regarding his estates arose. The numerous lands seized after his death constituted a very long list.

Hugh Courtenay, Earl of Devon, married Agnes; sister of John de St. John of Basing governor of Aquitaine and by her had a surviving son Hugh who would succeed his father as Earl of Devon.

HUGH COURTENAY, EARL OF DEVON

Hugh Courtenay was born 12 July 1303. Hugh, Earl of Devon, had accompanied his father on several military campaigns. Shortly after his father's death, Hugh, Earl of Devon received an order issued by King Edward III that directed him to travel to New Castle with sixty men-at-arms. The following year,

Hugh Courtenay accompanied King Edward III in an expedition into Brittany where Hugh led a garrison consisting of one banner followed by twelve knights, thirty-six esquires, and sixty archers on horseback. These forces took several castles and other strongholds that resisted them, and then King Edward's forces seized Vannes and conquered a large force led by Philip de Valois, which eventually led to a truce.

Because of Hugh's involvement during these military campaigns, he was known as "the warrior who drove the French back from their descent on Cornwall in 1339." (Burke's, p. 745.)

The numerous victories that Edward III now had won over France, as well as the blossoming of the new age of chivalry, led to the King's project for a Round Table in the manner of King Arthur. Several years following, the King led the first formal meeting of the "Noble Order of the Garter" or what is often called the "Knights of the Garter." Two stories exist about the foundation of the Order. The first takes place during a royal ball where Joan, Countess of Salisbury, supposedly dropped her garter and King Edward retrieved it and tied it around his own leg and said, in French, "shame on any who thinks evil of it." There are suggestions that this account is fiction and perhaps originated from the French Court. A more commonly accepted story is that the garter in question was a small strap used to attach various pieces of armor together and the thought was that the garter was used as a symbol of binding together in brotherhood; the motto reflected the leading political theme during the reign of Edward III's claim to the French throne.

The reason for the King's formation of the order will most likely remain obscured in time, but regardless of its origin, a Hugh Courtenay was among the original members and was present during the formation of the Order of the Garter.

Shortly thereafter, one of history's greatest natural disasters occurred: the Black Death. The bubonic plague eventually killed almost a third of the population of Europe and undermined the English economy; a large shortage of labor resulted.

For reasons that are unclear, Hugh Courtenay, Earl of Devon was informed that he would not accompany the King on a campaign into France. His brother-in-law the Earl of Northampton and his eldest son Hugh made a request to the King that Hugh Courtenay, Earl of Devon, be excused from attending Parliament or other Council meetings and the King granted their request. It was also at this time that Hugh, Earl of Devon, had requested a one-year leave of absence from the King and it was in that year that he built the house of White Friars in Fleet Street.

Hugh Courtenay, Earl of Devon, appeared as a witness for a receipt for monies paid to two knights for their services and later this same Hugh contributed the profits of the "market of the town of Tiverton" for the benefit of the poor of that parish. King Edward III then granted the same Hugh Courtenay permission to will all of his possessions in Devon and manors in other counties to his son, Philip.

Hugh, second Earl of Devon, married Margaret, daughter of Humphrey Bohun, Earl of Hereford and Essex and Lord High Constable of England. By Margaret, Hugh had sixteen children in a period when the child mortality rate was low and the financial responsibilities that these many children warranted was remarkable. They had seven sons and nine daughters.

There is a discrepancy in Mr. Cleaveland's genealogy of the Courtenay family during this generation; there is a Matilda mentioned in the family tree but the descriptive text refers to an Anne, and does not mention Matilda.

Nevertheless, of the seven sons it was Edward who would continue the direct ancestral line for the subject of this book.

EDWARD COURTENAY

Mr. Cleaveland fails to give any biographical information in his *A Genealogical History of the Noble and Illustrious Family of Courtenay*, about Edward Courtenay, son of Hugh, possibly for two reasons: first, it appears that Edward, son of Hugh Courtenay, died before his father, leaving Edward, son of Edward, son of Hugh, as heir. Thus, he may have chosen to overlook Hugh's son Edward in his genealogy because there was a lack of relevance. Second is the rather daunting (if not impossible) task of determining from historical records which Edward did what, when both were alive and only the name Edward Courtenay was used to identify them.

Mr. Cleaveland chronologically lists members of the Courtenay family in his book at this generation. The headings for these Edwards are:

"Chapter XII. Edward Courtenay, son of Edward Courtenay and Emlin, daughter of Sir John Dawney, grandson of Hugh, last Earl of Devon," and

"Chapter XIII. Edward Courtenay, eldest son of Edward, Earl of Devon, commonly called Edward Courtenay, Jr. to distinguish him from his father, son of Hugh."

None of the information that Mr. Cleaveland has included about these men coincides with the information provided in the illustration of the family tree. Fortunately, though it is certainly worthy of further investigation, the issue of "who was who" is beyond the scope of this book.

Burke's Peerage and Baronetage does give mention of Edward of Goodrington and mention of his marriage to Emmeline daughter of Sir J. Dawney, but that is all that is mentioned.

By her he had two sons, Edward and Hugh, later Hugh of Haccombe. Hugh Courtenay of Haccombe is directly related to the subject of this book, Edward Courtenay, as a great-great-great grandfather.

HUGH OF HACCOMBE

In the span of his lifetime, Hugh of Haccombe saw perhaps five monarchs on the throne. There are indications that he was with his uncle, Sir Philip Courtenay of Powderham during a campaign under the reign of King Richard II. Richard II was about ten years old when he succeeded his father (who was often regarded as the "Black Prince" because of his black armor). Richard's life has been described as an unhappy one with several bad omens that occurred at the beginning of his rather short reign. He is often described as possessing a lavish and profuse disposition; his subjects later revolted and raised arms against him and he was captured when he returned from Ireland. The circumstances of his death remain a matter of controversy, and the story inspired a play by Shakespeare and other dramatic writings.

During the reign of Henry V, Hugh of Haccombe served as Sheriff of Devonshire. King Henry V is described as an experienced soldier, a great politician, and highly proficient with the formation of plans and their execution that resulted in numerous successful campaigns of which it is possible that Hugh was involved in. King Henry V emphasized the rule of law and justice by following them himself and requiring others to do the same; he was regarded as a great Protector of the Church and clergy.

Sometimes over ambitious and not very liberal, he sometimes resorted to cruelty. King Henry V was another subject of Shakespeare's skillful pen.

Hugh of Haccombe married three times. His first wife was Elizabeth, daughter of Sir William Cogan of Baunton, and it was during his residency in Baunton that he was first called Sir Hugh Courtenay of Baunton. His second wife was Philippa, daughter and one of the co-heirs of Sir Warren Arcedekene of Haccombe, and by her, he had one daughter, Joan. It has been suggested that a portrait of a woman located in Haccombe Church, cut in gray marble, holding a book in her left hand and with her right hand on her breast, may in fact be the daughter of Hugh Courtenay.

History has not recorded the disposition of Hugh's first two wives, but it is through Hugh's third wife Matilda, daughter of Sir John Beaumont of Sherwell in Devon, that a son Hugh was born and would succeed his father in all honors and estates.

HUGH OF BOCONNOCK

Hugh of Boconnock was so named because of his residence in Cornwall; he has also been called Hugh Courtenay of Ashwater.

Hugh of Boconnock was involved in an interesting period of English history that began during the reign of King Henry VI (who became king at about nine months old). It has been said that he never really outgrew his childlike gentleness and naivety. Though his was a disastrous reign, his one personal achievement was the founding of King's College at Cambridge. Later in life, King Henry suffered what has been described as a complete mental collapse and Richard, Duke of York, assumed the duties of government. Henry eventually regained the throne but lost it again the following year; he fled to Scotland with his wife Margaret and their son Edward.

After a short time passed, Queen Margaret and Edward returned to England and were immediately greeted by Edmund, Earl of Somerset, John, Earl of Devon, and several others who welcomed them back. The Queen and her son then departed for Exeter, hoping to encourage others to join them in their campaign to place Henry back on the throne. Hugh of Boconnock and Sir John Arundel, accompanied by others they regarded as being trustworthy, rallied the counties of Devon and Cornwall to join the Queen when they marched to Tewkesbury where they fought a very bloody battle in 1471. The battle ended with Margaret taken prisoner, Prince Edward killed, and Edward IV ascended the throne. Hugh Courtenay was mortally wounded at the battle of Tewkesbury and there is a memorial in Tewkesbury Abbey in his honor.

His wife Margaret, daughter and co-heir of Thomas Carminow, survived Hugh. The Carminow family is said to be the most ancient in the county of Devon. A story has been passed down that a member of the Carminow family with his men opposed the landing of Julius Caesar.

Margaret had four daughters by Hugh, all married Cornish gentlemen, and two sons, Sir Walter and Edward. Edward would succeed his father in all honors and estates.

EDWARD, EARL OF DEVON

Edward Courtenay, son of Hugh of Boconnock, lived during what remains one of the most controversial periods in English history.

Following the death of Edward IV, the succession of his son Edward V was questioned and many felt that Richard, the Duke of Gloucester should have been placed on the throne instead. An accepted story is that Edward IV's marriage was contracted in adultery and as a result, his sons were bastards and were then placed under guard in the Tower. The fate of these two innocent young boys has been and will continue to be the subject of much conjecture even after several excavations and studies of bones found in the Tower. Many still believe that Richard of Gloucester, later known as Richard III, either murdered them or had them murdered and buried them under a stairway in the Tower.

These suspicions permanently tainted the reputation of Richard from early history onward though there are some indications that his short reign did reflect competence in governmental affairs. As the rumors and accusations against Richard increased, many people came to hate him, to a point that conspiracies against him began to flourish. Henry Stafford, Duke of Buckingham had been a very close friend of Richard of Gloucester before the controversial deaths of the two prince's and the accusations that followed, but he quickly switched sides and came up with plans to bring the exiled Henry Tudor to England to lead them.

Among the conspirators who joined with the Duke of Buckingham were Edward Courtenay, his brother Sir Walter Courtenay, Peter Courtenay, Bishop of Exeter, and several others. The Duke raised his army and was to later join forces with all those that the Courtenay's had acquired, but bad weather, bad organization, and gradual desertions reduced the campaign to a point that it failed; the Duke was captured and later beheaded. When word of this reached the forces they all fled, some of them to Brittany (where the Earl of Richmond was), including Edward Courtenay, Peter Courtenay, Bishop of Exeter, and Sir Walter Courtenay.

Soon after Richard III regained control, those who had contributed to his attempted disposal (about 500) were tried and found guilty of high treason, including Edward Courtenay, Peter Courtenay, and Sir Walter Courtenay. Richard may have regained control over his reign, but disaster soon followed when he lost his son and only heir to illness. It was not long after the loss of his son that he also lost his queen, and rumors that Richard had poisoned her with the intent to marry his niece were abundant.

With renewed interest and support, the Earl of Richmond with several gentlemen of importance in Wales, indicated that they were willing to assist the Earl in another campaign. With money, about 2000 men, and a couple of ships, the Earl arrived in the harbor of Milford with the Earl of Oxford, Peter Courtenay, Bishop of Exeter, Edward Courtenay, and several other gentlemen who fled England after the first unsuccessful campaign against King Richard.

A fierce battle occurred between Henry, Earl of Richmond, and King Richard's forces with causalities on both sides. During the battle, Richard's horse was killed, right out from under him, leaving him without a mount. This is supposed to be the origin of the famous saying that has been passed down through history, "A horse, a horse, my kingdom for a horse."

King Richard received mortal wounds and history has recorded that he died courageously in battle. The Earl of Richmond was immediately crowned Henry VII with the very crown that was removed from Richard's head. The new king was quick to reward those who had supported him; and among those were Edward Courtenay who was then created the Earl of Devon on 26 October 1485. The title included all honors, boroughs, and manors including Plympton and Okehampton, the castle and manor of Tiverton, the manors of Sampford-Courtenay, Chaverleigh, Cornwood, and Norton-Damerel, numerous additional manors, and 3 mills. King Henry also gave him governorship of Kesterwell in Cornwall and made him one of the Knights of the Garter.

Several years later, Edward, Earl of Devon accompanied King Henry VII on a campaign into France. The King, feeling that war with France was necessary, gathered an estimated twenty-five thousand infantrymen and sixteen hundred soldiers on horse. Thomas, Marquess of Dorset, Thomas, Earl of Arundel, Edward, Earl of Devon, and many other earls, barons, and knights were included in this army. Commissioners sent ahead of the army were successful in securing a treaty before a battle had taken place and King Henry withdrew back to England. Many were disappointed that no battle had occurred.

A few years following that campaign, a gentleman who some suggest was Perkin Warbeck mustered an estimated three to four thousand men and landed in England then proclaimed himself Richard IV in 1497. King Henry responded quickly, but in the meantime Edward, Earl of Devon, his son William Courtenay of Powderham, Sir Edward Carew, Sir Thomas Trenchard, Sir Thomas Fulford, Sir John Hallewell, Sir John Croker, and Sir Walter Courtenay assisted the citizens of Exeter in stopping the advancement of Warbeck's forces and Warbeck then withdrew and was soon after captured and then later hanged. Edward Courtenay received a wound by an arrow in his arm during the assault.

Edward Courtenay, Earl of Devon, married Elizabeth, daughter of Sir Philip Courtenay of Molland, and by her had a son and heir, William.

WILLIAM COURTENAY, EARL OF DEVON

William Courtenay married Catherine, the sixth daughter of King Edward IV. This rather interesting branch of the Courtenay family tree produced several remarkable marriages. (Edward IV also had a daughter Elizabeth, who married King Henry VII of England and had two surviving children, Henry VIII and Mary, grandmother of Lady Jane Grey, who reigned for nine days in July of 1553. The other child of Edward IV was Edward V who, as mentioned earlier, was murdered by Richard III.)

Towards the end of the reign of Henry VII, Edmund de la Pole, Earl of Suffolk, his mother and Lady Elizabeth sister of King Edward IV, led a rebellion against King Henry VII. After the rebellion failed, Edmund fled to Flanders to his aunt, the Lady Margaret, Duchess of Burgundy, for safety. King Henry VII was not at first aware that Edmund fled England, but King Henry soon sent a man to locate him.

King Henry VII, through various means, discovered that some individuals had plotted against him and he acquired their names. Many were taken prisoner including William Courtenay, Lord William de le Pole, Sir James Tyrell, and Sir John Wyndham. William Courtenay and Lord William de la Pole were only held on suspicion because they were close in kin to the conspirator. William Courtenay's marriage into the royal family was very unfortunate for him as King Henry VII kept him in prison for the remainder of his reign. Sir John Tyrrel and Sir John Wyndham were convicted of high treason and later were beheaded on Tower Hill.

History has recorded that Henry VII was a thoroughly medieval king, and his reign was filled with rebellions. He was regarded as brave, wise, and prudent. His command of government was strong and his decisions were sensible and served justice. He was valiant in battle though some indications show that he preferred peace. King Henry VII died in the same year that Edward Courtenay, Earl of Devon, father of William Courtenay, died. Upon the King's death, William Courtenay received his freedom when King Henry VIII acceded to the throne and William bore the third sword at the King's coronation.

On New Year's Day of the following year, the Queen gave birth to a boy, but he only lived about two months. Preparations were made to honor the Queen with jousting tournaments with King Henry VIII and three others: William Courtenay, Earl of Devon, Sir Thomas Nevet, and Sir Edward Nevil. These events lifted the Queen's spirits.

Later that year the King had another royal ceremony that lasted for three days and included more jousting matches. Following a lavish banquet, the Queen gave the chief prize to the King, the second to the Earl of Essex, and the third to William Courtenay, Earl of Devon. The following year William, Earl of Devon, contracted a pleurisy fever, which has been described as being rare at the time and his physicians were unskilled in resolving the illness. The Earl died.

Although the King had drawn up the letters that secured William Courtenay the title of Earl of Devon, his body remained in the King's Court at Greenwich for three days until the King commanded that his burial should be that of a nobleman. His burial occurred on the south side of the alter at Paul's Church.

His wife Catherine, daughter of Edward IV, survived William, Earl of Devon. Catherine gave him a daughter Margaret, and a story was once told that Margaret died very young as a result of choking on a fish bone at Colecomb and that the monument of an antique figure that remained at the parish church of Colyton was in memory of her, but this is now believed not to be true and the monument is that of Margaret Beaufort wife of

Thomas de Courtenay. Catherine also had a son Henry, who received all his father's honors and estates.

HENRY COURTENAY, MARQUESS OF EXETER

At the age of 17, Henry Courtenay served as second captain of a man-of-war in a naval campaign against France in 1513.

When the King and Queen of France visited England, large crowds gathered to watch as King Henry VIII and the King of France entered the field in fabulous ornate armor and issued a challenge to anyone who wished to joust. Henry Courtenay rode forward accepting the challenge, and then charged the King of France; the King responded in kind. As they rode full speed towards each other, their spears made contact with the other's chest and broke into pieces, which caused the crowd to roar with approval. For Christmas in 1521, while at Greenwich, the King and Henry Courtenay challenged anyone at arms and sixteen men responded, but the King won at each event. When the Emperor Charles V of Spain visited England, there were many jousting tournaments in honor of the occasion. The King and Henry Courtenay were placed against the Duke of Suffolk and the Marquess of Dorset and during this display, Henry Courtenay fought valiantly.

Later in that same year, Henry Courtenay met the King and Queen of Denmark at Dover and escorted them to London to be received by King Henry VIII and the Queen in grand splendor. King Henry VIII made Henry Courtenay the Marquess of Exeter on 18 June 1525, and he was one of the commissioners of the King of England in a treaty designed for the redemption of Francis I, King of France, who was at the time being held prisoner by the Emperor Charles V. Later that same year, King Henry VIII was accompanied by the Duke of Suffolk, the Duke of Norfolk, the

Marquess of Dorset, and Henry Courtenay to meet King Francis I, but before they were to meet, King Henry VIII nominated Henry Courtenay his "heir apparent to the crown" in the event something should happen to him.

Soon after, Elizabeth I was born at Greenwich. The christening occurred in the Fryer Church where the procession contained the Earl of Essex carrying the covered basin gilt, Henry Courtenay carrying a taper of virgin-wax, and the Marquess of Dorset bearing salt. When the ceremonies were completed, the archbishop gave Elizabeth a standing cup of gold and Henry Courtenay gave three bowls beautifully engraved and overlaid in gilt and covers.

Henry Courtenay, Marquess of Exeter, served as a commissioner on the jury in the trial of Anne Boleyn.

Later that same year a riot began in Yorkshire. With estimates at about forty thousand rioters, King Henry VIII was quick to react by sending the Duke of Norfolk, his lieutenant-general, Henry Courtenay, the Earl of Shrewsbury, the Earl of Huntington, and the Earl of Rutland with an army to stand against the rioters.

The Earl of Shrewsbury, the Earl of Huntington, and the Earl of Rutland gathered their forces from the counties of Shrewsbury, Stafford, and Leicester. Shortly after the Duke of Norfolk arrived with his forces, Henry Courtenay arrived with forces consisting mostly of western men. The battle did not occur because of bad weather and the rebels requested a pardon from the King, which the Duke of Norfolk promised they would receive and which King Henry did eventually grant.

Late in the same year, Henry Courtenay, along with Henry Pole, Lord Montague, and Sir Edward Nevil were imprisoned in the Tower of London, accused by Sir Jeoffry Poole of allegedly committing high treason. It has been suggested that Thomas

Cromwell discovered that in Cornwall "a painted banner had been made which was to be carried round the villages, rousing the men to rebel against the crown in order to declare Courtenay heir-apparent to the throne." [Burke's, 746]

At his trial, Henry Courtenay is quoted as saying, "I like well of the proceedings of Cardinal Pole, but I like not the proceedings of this realm; and I trust to see a change of the world: I trust once to have a fair day upon these knaves which rule about the King; I trust to give them a buffet one day." That statement certainly has overtones of disaffection towards Protestantism that Henry VIII stood so firmly behind, as Cardinal Pole represented the Catholic faith.

A tale has survived that says an old man in Tiverton, in Devonshire, informed the Marquess that on a specified day, the King would send men to capture him and remove his head if the Marquess did not leave quickly. When that day came the Marquess told the old man that he was a lunatic and a false prophet. The old man replied, "Sir, there is a party of horsemen now coming to seize you, and they are come within a half a mile of the town." Henry Courtenay, convinced that the old man was a lunatic, did not heed his warnings to leave quickly and Courtenay was soon captured and imprisoned.

The four men were indicted for devising to maintain, promote, and advance Reginald Pole, the late Dean of Exeter, and to remove the King from the throne. On 3 December, they were tried before a Council of their peers, found guilty, and beheaded on the Tower Hill. A session of Parliament soon followed and among the issues discussed was to what extent the Marchioness of Exeter and the Countess of Sarum were involved with Sir Nicholas Carew in his treasonous acts. The Marchioness was not executed because she was not of a royal bloodline, but she was placed in the Tower with her son Edward to prevent the possibility of any further treasonous acts either by them or by their devise.

Henry Courtenay, the Earl of Devon, married twice but had no children by his first wife, Elizabeth. His second marriage was to Gertrude, daughter of William Blount, Lord Montjoy, and she gave birth to two children: Henry, who died young, and Edward, the subject of this biography.

CHAPTER 2. 1526-JULY 1553. KING HENRY VIII AND EDWARD VI

There are no known or surviving documents that would help establish the precise date of birth for Edward Courtenay, the Earl of Devon, but it is generally believed to have been during the year 1526 in Okehampton, Devonshire, England during the reign of Henry VIII.

There are no known surviving documents that would give some insight to Edward's childhood, but the Courtenay family's long held social prominence (they are often regarded as the richest and most influential family in Devon in the Middle Ages and Tudor period) would have ensured that Edward received a good education. It would be safe to speculate that his childhood was somewhat sheltered and his exposure to other children his age would have been limited to those of a similar social level, presumably rather few in number.

His education most likely would have been a combination of tutors and members of his family who would have determined the course of his studies. It has been suggested that Dr. Thomas Wylson, later Secretary of State, may have been one of his tutors.

Beyond the fundamental subjects of arithmetic, reading, and writing taught to most upper class children of the period, his studies would have included several languages, including Latin, in order to provide a fundamental understanding of the classics and there is a good chance that he was exposed to Spanish, Italian, or French — which was the language of his ancestors. It appears that he understood and conversed in these languages with a comfortable level of proficiency. Later in life, he would travel to several different countries and possessing these tools certainly would have helped him.

In addition to his study of languages, it has been suggested that his studies of mathematics indicated a mind capable of problem solving and logical reasoning and the same sources mention his talent in the arts and his works showed that a tutor who recognized these talents would most likely have cultivated these abilities.

Other talents included the ability to compose and perform on various musical instruments such as the guitar and lute, which produced results that were comparable to his accomplishments in art.

Because of the Courtenay family's high social status, his childhood would also have included exposure to the activities of the Court. He was born during the period when Catherine was Queen, but a young Anne Boleyn, maid of honor to the Queen, quickly caught the eye of Henry VIII. Very soon afterwards, Henry began proceedings for a divorce from Catherine after a marriage of about 20 years. A divorce during this period, especially in the royal family, made for a great deal of controversy and caused the downfall of Cardinal Thomas Wolsey, who opposed it. With the support of several universities, both local and abroad, Henry VIII composed a letter to the pope in 1530. Opposition from Rome was to be expected and continued for several years, straining the relations between the two sovereign bodies.

Determined to have his own way regardless of the church's lack of support, Henry secretly married Anne Boleyn and she became pregnant soon after the marriage. Through further persuasions, the marriage between Catherine and Henry was finally annulled and the marriage between Anne and Henry was ratified. To add to their bliss, they were soon blessed with a daughter, Elizabeth.

The year 1534 saw Henry's final breach with Rome as the marriage to Catherine was nullified and her daughter Mary removed from the order of succession to the throne. Henry VIII further agitated Rome by performing several executions of those whose views were different from his own.

The following year saw the illness and death of Queen Catherine. Her affection for Henry had not changed even though he had cast her aside, and she had cared for him a great deal as her surviving letters clearly indicate.

Anne Boleyn fell out of the King's favor when she delivered a stillborn son. King Henry's strong desire for a male heir caused his temper to flare and he demanded that the innocent mother answer for the misfortune. His affection quickly turned to Jane, daughter of Sir John Seymour, and Anne was sent to the Tower of London, protesting her innocence in vain. A jury consisting of the Duke of Suffolk, the Marquess of Exeter, and twenty-four others tried the Queen and her brother. Anne prepared for death as Henry dissolved the marriage. He began preparation for his marriage to Jane Seymour soon after Anne's execution in 1536.

In 1538, upon the arrest of his father on a charge of high treason, Edward Courtenay, then at about the age of 12 or 13, and his mother the Marchioness of Exeter, were placed in the Tower as prisoners. Though Courtenay and his mother had not actually committed any crimes themselves, King Henry VIII took no chances that either of them could take up the cause which Henry Courtenay had started. With Courtenay and his mother inside the secure walls of the Tower, their actions, visitors, and daily activities could be closely monitored.

The same year saw many changes in the kingdom. The rebellions of the past couple of years over the control of the monasteries had been suppressed and the birth of son Edward made Henry finally rejoice that the throne would stay within the Tudor family. Henry's joy was quickly quenched by the death of the Queen two days after she gave birth.

The treasures of the churches were now being confiscated and often destroyed in front of large crowds of people. Other property of the churches became the sole possession of the King. The following year Parliament met and among the various issues placed before them was the fate of the Marchioness of Exeter and her possible involvement with Sir Nicholas Carew in his treasonous acts against King Henry. It appears that no witnesses were examined or testimonies recorded against the Marchioness and because she was not related by blood to the family Courtenay, she was eventually released from the confinement of the Tower, leaving behind her young son Courtenay to remain within the confines of the Tower walls for the reminder of Henry's reign.

It would be safe to speculate that during the next six to seven years as a prisoner in the Tower, Courtenay would have continued his educational studies through the reading of any books that were available, writing, and by visitors bringing news of events in the outside world. He would have most likely continued to play musical instruments, compose poetry, and do anything to occupy his mind during the long hours in confinement. Though he was able to expand his intelligence, he was missing the social skills that a person of his age and family social status should have been experiencing through activities in Court, which would hinder him later in life.

During Courtenay's confinement, it has been suggested that he was allowed to spend time engaged in activities with the lieutenant of the Tower's children in the Tower gardens. However, as he grew older, he was guarded more strictly and closely confined in the Belfry Tower in a room that overlooked the river.

King Henry VIII never reevaluated Courtenay's case, possibly fearing his involvement in another plot against him if he were to be released. In Henry's remaining years, he grew obese and restricted by his hugely swollen legs. His vices had caught up with him and his popularity was at its lowest ever during his long reign. The tragedies and scandals he had created, such as the abolishment of the churches and keeping their treasures for himself and perverting the rights of religion, marriage, faith, and promise had reduced a once great king to one that many called a tyrant. Henry's last hours were spent in bed fading in and out of consciousness, worried more about forgiveness for his sins than the state of the kingdom as he prepared for death, which occurred in the early hours of Friday, 28 January 1547.

The fruits of his six marriages had produced one prince, Edward, and two princesses, Mary and Elizabeth. Edward would succeed him.

Edward's coronation was glorious and filled with the splendor one would expect of a Renaissance monarch. Many accounts of the ceremony paint a vivid image but it appears that young Edward was rather indifferent to such pageantries. With the official ceremonies over, it was time to begin addressing the issues of state.

In the beginning of Edward VI's reign, the kingdom was divided with religious disputes which were carried on with such violence and inveteracy that the spirit of persecution was very prevalent even among the Protestants, though they greatly con-demned the Catholics for it. Though Edward VI was in fact the successor to the throne and King of England, he was at the time only about nine years old and not able to undertake the full responsibilities on his own until the age of eighteen, and the late King Henry VIII had provisions in place to address this by assigning sixteen executors that were entrusted with the gov-ernment of the king and kingdom. These gentlemen's names were: Cranmer, Archbishop of Canterbury; Lord Wriothesely, Chancellor; Lord St. John, Great Master; Dr. Wotton, Dean of Canterbury; Sir Edward Wotton, Treasurer of Calais; Sir William Herbert, Chief Gentlemen of the Privy Chamber; Sir Anthony Denny; Judge Bromley; Sir Edward North, Chancellor of the Court of Augmentations; Sir Edward Montague, Chief Justice of the Common Pleas; Sir William Paget, Secretary of the State; Sir Anthony Brown, Master of the Horse; Tonstal, Bishop of Durham; Viscount Lisle, Admiral; Lord Russell, Privy Seal; and the Earl of Hertford, Chamberlain.

To these executors were appointed twelve counselors who possessed no real power and could only assist by supplying advice if required. These gentlemen were: the Earls of Arundel and Essex; Sir Thomas Sheney, Treasurer of the Household; Sir John Gage, Comptroller; Sir Anthony Wingfield, Vice Cham-berlain; Sir William Petre, Secretary of State; Sir Richard Rich; Sir John Baker; Sir Ralph Sadler; Sir Thomas Seymour; Sir Richard Southwell; and Sir Edmund Peckham. Among the first issues that the executors and counselors were to address was to assign one person who would represent the new king in affairs of state and serve as a Protector. Chancellor Wriothesely felt that he was best qualified for the task, but he was not a popular choice and it was decided that the Earl of Hertford would serve as Protector because he was the King's maternal uncle and would have the King's best interest at heart. Soon after, Hertford was created Duke of Somerset, Mareschal, and Lord Treasurer. Other men were also granted or advanced in rank as promised by the late King Henry VIII in his will. King Henry felt that the creation of nobility for those who deserved it for various reasons (such as giving faithful service to the king and kingdom) would ensure their loyalty to the crown.

With King Edward VI now firmly seated on the throne and most of the primary issues addressed regarding the matters of state, the young king addressed the prisoners in the Tower as most monarchs do when first settled on the throne. On 19 February 1547, the young king pardoned and released all those who were confined during his late father's reign except six. Among those who remained in the Tower were Cardinal Pole, the Duke of Norfolk, and Edward Courtenay. Though each case of those remaining confined in the Tower were as different as the individuals themselves and though some were innocent, King Edward VI was advised that they were best left as prisoners and could possibly jeopardize the security of the state if these suspicious individuals were to be released. Most certainly, Courtenay's hopes for freedom must have run high upon learning of the death of Henry VIII that his freedom may be granted by the new monarch. Unfortunately, Courtenay would not gain his liberty for another six years, punished for nothing he had done himself.

It was not long after that the once subjected partisans of both religions and the hopes of the Protestants and the fears of the Catholics began to revive with the new monarch. The zeal of these parties produced disputes and animosities that were once suppressed by the tyrannical Henry VIII. As tutors were put in place to educate the new king, those of the Catholic faith feared his views towards Protestantism because he considered abolishing the Catholic faith in England. Nevertheless, this would not be the case, as Edward was more lenient than his father was and some of the old faith was allowed to be preserved. Nevertheless, a reformation was in progress that had actually become violent in Scotland and it was decided that rigorous punishments should be brought against the reformers to serve as an example to those who may decide to rise in the future.

As the Protector began preparations for war against Scotland, he issued a manifesto to Scotland hoping to prevent war. Included in the manifesto was a statement that "nature seemed originally to have intended this island for one empire." The Protector included this line, hoping to promote unity. The Protector also recommended a union by marriage of their Queen dowager to Edward VI. Regardless of the Protector's efforts to prevent it, a battle did in fact come to be. At first, the English army was met by a wall of Scottish infantry and could not advance forward. With the assistance of the English ships stationed in the harbor, the Protector, assisted by Sir Ralph Sadle and Sir Ralph Vane, positioned their cavalry and artillery in strategic positions. This caused the Scots to retreat, leaving behind a bloody trail of bodies, as the English were relentless in their vengeance. Some accounts of the battle indicate that the English lost only about 300 men and the Scots lost about 10,000 with 1500 taken prisoner. This encounter was called the Battle of Pinkey.

Upon his return to England, the Protector summoned a Parliament and in this session, repeals of several of the most rigorous laws that had ever been passed in England were annulled. Other laws were passed including civil and religious liberties and there were numerous other changes made. All were regarded as major turning points in English history and as the year 1547 closed, more changes were in progress that would reshape England and how others would regard the nation. The reign of Henry VIII was truly over.

The Protector, though having successfully changed several laws, was still troubled by one unsolved thorn in his side, the Scots, and he offered a truce whereupon they insisted on the return of the places that were taken from them. No resolve came from this and minor skirmishes occurred as a result.

Perhaps motivated by the changes in religious policies, Edward Courtenay, still a prisoner in the Tower, translated a 1543 Italian version of the *Trattato* (Treaty) into English. He presented the completed manuscript to the Duchess of Somerset, wife of the Protector, including a prayer for her to exert her powerful influence in his favor to promote his release from confinement. King Edward VI reviewed this copy perhaps after the Duchess reviewed it, as his autograph is at both ends of the volume.

The *Trattato* was read and enjoyed in several countries such as Italy, Germany, France, and Spain either in the original dialect or in the dialect of the country. It is estimated that about fifty thousand original copies were printed, an astonishing number considering how primitive printing was at the time, but the originals seem to have all but vanished.

A description of this treasure is as follows: The manuscript is beautifully written on fine vellum, and consists of 92 leaves, each of which is 3 ¼ inches high by 2 3/8 inches broad, unpaged; the pages contain about 18 lines each, and are bordered on three (sometimes on four) sides with two straight lines of gold, having a straight silver line between them. The headings and first lines of the chapters are in gold, and the initial letters of the chapters are enclosed in a small square of bright blue, ornamented with gold sprigs. The title page is written in gold, in a character resembling Roman type, ornamented with scrollwork also in gold and looks like this:

A TREATICE
Most profitable of
the benefitte that true
christianes receyue
by the dethe
of
IESVS CHRISTE.
1548. [Bell & Daldy]

The reverse side of the title page begins the dedication, which occupies nearly six pages. The dedication reads, "To the right virtuous lady and gratious Princes Anne Duches of Somerset, Edwarde Courtenay the sorrofull captive are wisheth all honor & felicite." The next page is blank, except that it contains the words; "Faith is dede if it be without workes. Your loving neueu Edward." The penultimate page similarly only has the words "Liue to die and die to lieu again. Your neueu Edward."

The last and antepenultimate pages are wholly blank. It has been indicated that the marginal notes in the Italian copy have been omitted. The Scripture references are also disregarded in the manuscript and have been mutilated by the careless knife of the bookbinder and are not readable.

It would be safe to speculate that Courtenay spent a great deal of time translating this manuscript. There were few things to occupy his time other than study and an occasional visitor and a stimulating project such as this was would surely be a welcome change to the mundane Tower life. It would also be safe to speculate that Courtenay was rather industrious and this most certainly was not the only project of this type that he undertook during his 15 years of imprisonment, though no other has surfaced. This project could most certainly give evidence to the language skills that Courtenay possessed.

The year 1549 saw further reforms in various religious policies that included Parliament enacting a law allowing priests to marry and forbidding the use of flesh meat during Lent and other periods of abstinence. Many in the kingdom still remained devoted to the old religious ways, including the Lady Mary, who adhered to Mass and refused to admit the established modes of worship.

Other problems were beginning to form in the kingdom as the common people began to complain how impoverished they were in comparison to other European countries and how the average wage still remained at rates established long ago. The protector quickly acted upon the complaints of the common people and attempted to address their concerns, but the Council quickly suppressed him. The common people feared that the issue would be forever avoided and they sought a remedy by a force of arms with several risings in several counties. Many rioters were killed in the field and some were executed by martial law. This quieted the actions in some of the smaller counties but other risings flared elsewhere.

Many took the opportunity to incorporate their various religious grievances and took up arms, but the leaders were quickly apprehended and sent to London where they were tried and executed. Others were executed under martial law, including the Vicar of St. Thomas who was hanged on the top of his own steeple. These actions helped to bring the situation under control.

The Protector soon found himself totally alienated by his own counselors, and others soon followed. They indicated that he had not followed the conditions of the agreement for his position that were set forth in which he should act only act on their advice and direction, of which he did not, and he soon found himself a prisoner in the same Tower he had sent so many to on his own judgment. A session of Parliament was held and the Protector was prevailed on to confess on his knees, which he did. Convicted of a misdemeanor, he was removed from all of the offices that he held and a fine was imposed that was later remitted by King Edward. Then he was granted liberty and the Earl of Warwick assumed some of his responsibilities. As a result of the riots, an important law was passed indicating that if a riot formed consisting of more than twelve people who would not disperse if requested to do so by any authority figure, it would be regarded as an act of treason and punishable as such.

Peace with Scotland and France allowed other ambitions to be pursued. The Earl of Warwick seized several opportunities to receive the young king's favor and was granted the Duke of Northumberland. His ambitions led him to acquire various possessions of titles and among those he targeted was the Duke of Somerset, whom he had set out to ruin. In retaliation, Somerset often displayed anger towards Northumberland's intimidations and, with information received by a spy that Northumberland placed near to Somerset, received information that the Duke of Somerset wanted to murder him.

Northumberland jumped at the opportunity presented to him and the Duke of Somerset and several others including Sir Ralph Vane and the Duchess of Somerset were arrested and confined in the Tower. Somerset was brought to trial and the Duke of Northumberland was among the twenty-seven members of the jury. The Duke of Somerset was accused of high treason because of the projected insurrections and of a felony entreating to murder privy counselors (Northumberland). The charge of treason was dropped as a result of a good defense, but the felony charge would condemn him to death.

The year 1552 began with the execution of Somerset and several others involved, including Sir Ralph Vane, on the scaffold on Tower Hill. The day after the executions a session of Parliament was held and further advances were made towards the establishment of the reformation. Among the concerns addressed by Parliament was that the King and his successor, the Lady Mary, were professedly of different religions and under a new law anyone who spoke against the King would be guilty of treason. This law was rejected, rewritten, and then passed in the House of Peers.

The young King Edward VI was soon plagued with the increasing debts of the crown, which at the time were considerable, and of his own declining health. First overcome with the measles, he recovered but was then afflicted with a cough that proved obstinate and resistant to medicine. Soon symptoms of consumption appeared, causing great concern. In early February 1553, the King came down with a feverish cold. He did not recover as he had from other illnesses in the past, and on March 1, he was forced to open a new session of Parliament in the great chamber of Whitehall instead of at Westminster. Later the young king was unable to go to Greenwich for Easter as he had hoped, it was described that he was still troubled with catarrh and a cough. News of Edward's illness, which was now more severe than his past ailments, spread quickly through the kingdom. Many, including his own physicians, feared that the Lord would take him from them soon. The once vibrant and active king was confined to his bed where he grew weaker with each passing day.

In the second week of April, Edward felt well enough to move to Greenwich and though he remained weak, he made a public appearance in the gardens the day after he arrived. It was at about this point that the over ambitious Duke of Northumberland, though not able to attain a higher level of social status himself, devised a plan. The first part of this plan was to marry his only unwed son Guildford to Lady Jane Grey, daughter of Henry Grey, Duke of Suffolk. Following that, Northumberland would devise a way to place Lady Jane on the throne. The late King Henry VIII's will indicated that the first to succeed him would of course be Edward, then Mary and Elizabeth. After the Lady Elizabeth were the daughters of the Duchess of Suffolk, the eldest being Lady Jane, then Catherine and Mary. After the heirs of the daughters of the Duchess of Suffolk would be the Countess of Cumberland and then Edward Courtenay, Earl of Devon. Mary, Queen of Scots, was overlooked because of her foreign affairs.

Northumberland's plan involved rewording the will of the late King Henry VIII and alter the order of succession based in part on the little known fact that Parliament had already declared the marriages of Henry VIII to Katherine of Aragon and Anne Boleyn illegitimate. This made their daughters, the Lady Mary and the Lady Elizabeth, bastards and invalidated their claim to the crown. Next to remove was Mary, Queen of Scots, and then Frances Grey, the Duchess of Suffolk, because of her age. Finally, the rewording would place the Lady Jane on the throne.

In The Chronicle of Queen Jane, John G. Nichols points out the change in wording in Edward's devise: "The next alternative was to appoint the Lady Jane to be the positive heir to the throne. This was actually done by altering the words in his will from "...to the L' Jane's heires masles" to "to the L' Jane and her heires masles." Nichols further indicates that in the King's devise, a pen line is drawn through the letter "s," which remains on the paper, and the words "and her" are written above the line.

Lady Jane's parents were very persuasive and overcame her objections to marriage, and as her wedding date set for May 21 approached, Edward's physicians announced that he was too weak to be present. Edward's deep affection and high regard for his cousin made his inability to attend difficult for him. A surviving quotation describes the wedding ceremony as "a gaudy glittering parade conducted, to Ascham's disgust, 'much in the old popish fashion' and he added, which was later to be proved correct, that John Dudley, 'notwithstanding his pretended zeal for the Reformation, was a papist at heart' " [Lindsay 137].

In early June, Edward's doctors told the Spanish Ambassador that the King would not live more than three days; Northumberland's plan depended on the King living longer. Though Edward's devise was in rough draft, it needed to be completed and passed through Parliament. The Duke could not do that if Edward died and realized that he must act quickly.

The imperial Ambassador Scheyfue in his letter of 11 June 1553 mentioned the earliest suggestion of a marriage between Courtenay and Princess Mary. In this letter, the Ambassador also mentions that Courtenay would be eliminated from those considered for marriage to the Princess by some means that is not mentioned. There is some indication that the thought of murdering Courtenay had crossed the minds of some, not necessarily for what he had done but what he could do if placed on the throne in the future, though as a prisoner confined in the Tower, Courtenay could not do a great deal of anything. This same Ambassador mentions that the Duke of Northumberland was said to be planning to murder his present wife by the use of poison and then to ally himself with Princess Mary.

The Lord Chief Justice, Sir Edward Montague, the Solicitor-General, and the Attorney General were summoned to Greenwich palace on 12 June. They arrived to find Edward still in bed with a persistent cough, attended by Northumberland and several Councilors. The judges each knelt at the royal bedside then waited for the King to speak. In a raspy voice, Edward addressed the judges:

> "Our long sickness hath caused us heavily to think of the conditions and prospects of our realm. Should the Lady Mary or the Lady Elizabeth succeed, she might marry a stranger, and the laws and liberties of England be sacrificed, and religion changed. We desire, therefore, that the succession be altered, and we call upon your Lordships to receive our command upon the drawing up of this deed by letters patent." [Chapman, The Last Tutor King, 180]

When the King finished, he ordered the judges to draw up a deed of settlement upon its articles. Cautious with his response, the Lord Chief Justice said, "What His Majesty requires is illegal and could not be drawn up under the heading of an act of Parliament." To this Edward replied, "I will hear no objections. I command you to draw the letters patient forthwith" as he was coughing and gasping for breath. The judges were certainly in a dilemma. They realized that the King's command was illegal, but if they did not do as he ordered it could be regarded as an act of treason. After carefully considering their options, the judges requested time to review the document and Edward gave his approval.

The Council informed the judges that they would meet at Northumberland's Palace of Ely Place in Holborn. The judges were divided as some were willing to do as the King has ordered, some unwilling to proceed with this illegal command, and some were just uncertain what they should do. A member of the Council asked Sir Edward Montague whether he had agreed to sign the devise or not, he responded that he could not do so. Suddenly a door flew open startling everyone, and Northumberland burst in trembling in anger and called Sir Edward Montague a traitor.

The following day, the judges reluctantly returned to an angry Edward, still confined in his bed but still very much in command of the situation. Northumberland was present with members of the Privy Council all surrounding Edwards's bed. Having already been briefed by Northumberland, Edward then asked the judges in a sharp and raspy voice where his letter of patent was and why they had not signed it as he had commanded. After listening to their pathetic reasons, the King ordered Sir Edward Montague to "make quick dispatch" and added that he intended to call a session of Parliament to ratify the document immediately. Montague, now sobbing, fell to his knees and pleaded with the King: "I have served Your Majesty and Your Majesty's noble father these nineteen years. I am a weak old man without comfort and with nineteen children."

Edward, still frustrated and upset, ignored Montague's pleas and repeated his order. After much discussion, the King and the judges eventually agreed that all who signed the devise would be pardoned, and with that, they all reluctantly signed.

Having completed the first step of his plan by making the King alter his fathers will, Northumberland then used intimidating tactics to those who were stubborn and rewards to those who supported him in the form of land grants to members of the Council to ensure their signing of the King's document. By 21 June, the judges and the Privy Council had all signed the devise.

Edward's illness grew worse with each passing day and the Duke of Northumberland realized he must keep the King alive long enough to apprehend Mary, who would most certainly assert her claim to the crown when her brother died. Northumberland dismissed the physicians who had tended the King since his birth and replaced them with his own doctor and a woman (early historians suggest she was a schoolmistress) who claimed that she could restore the King's health to normal. Disregarding the vehement complaints by Edward's physicians, a woman with no demonstrable professional skills and of unknown reputation gained complete access to the King of England. Within a period of a couple of days, the remedies she employed began to take a toll on the King as they contained small quantities of arsenic and made Edward's hair fall out and darkened his once pale skin. Many now questioned the woman's motives and in early July, she was dismissed and never heard from again. There are suggestions that she was murdered to keep her silent. Edward's own physicians were then allowed access to the King and quickly attempted to undo what the woman had done as rumors quickly flourished that the Duke of Northumberland and his accomplice were intentionally poisoning the King.

Eagar crowds gathered on 2 and 3 July to see their King, but a gentleman from Edward's bedchamber told them the air was too cold for Edward and he would visit them when it has warmed up a little.

The Duke of Northumberland's reputation had been damaged by the rumors of poison and the unorthodox choice of a schoolmistress to treat the King. Whether or not the Duke did attempt to poison Edward is debatable, but it is clear that since the King had signed the devise Northumberland had no further need for Edward. In a letter from John Burcher to Henry Bullinger dated 16 August 1553, Burcher attempts to reflect the feelings of many, including "learned men." This letter provides matter for further debate.

> Greeting. What I wrote in my formal letter, my honored Bullinger, is daily confirmed, and more than confirmed, by the statements of some excellent men. That monster of a man, the Duke of Northumberland, has been committing a horrible and portentous crime. A writer worthy of credit informs me, that our excellent King has been most shamefully taken off by poison. His nails and hair fell off before his death, so that, handsome as he was, he entirely lost all his good looks. The perpetrators of the murder were ashamed of allowing the body of the deceased King to lie in state, and be seen by the public, as is usual: wherefore they buried

him privately in a paddock adjoining the palace, and substituted in his place, to be seen by the people, a youth not very unlike him whom they had murdered. One of the sons of the Duke of Northumberland acknowledged this fact. The Duke has been apprehended with his five sons, and nearly twenty persons of rank: among whom are Master Cheke, Doctor Cox, and the Bishop of London, with others unknown to you by either name or reputation. It is thought that these persons gave their consent and sanction, that Jane, the wife of the Duke's son, should be proclaimed Queen: should this prove to be the case, it is all over with them. The King of France has sent word to the city of Calais and to Guisnes, for the citizens to remove, and leave the city and camp at Guisnes at his disposal, for that it was promised him by the English Council. The Duke and his fellow prisoners are supposed to have been guilty of this shameful deed. Forces are collecting in England to defend the city and territory. I am afraid lest your Swiss should be sent against us. You see, my dear friend, how you are deprived of all your expectation respecting our England: you must consider therefore what you should determine upon respecting your son. My house is open to him, and my services shall not be wanting. Farewell, and diligently, I pray you, salute all your learned men. I am exceedingly obliged to you all for the kindness you have shewn me.

Yours, BURCHER. [Robinson 104].

Edward, the last Tudor King, died in the arms of Doctor Sidney between eight and nine o'clock on the evening of 6 July uttering these last words: "I am faint: Lord have mercy upon me, and take my spirit."

It was decided that Edward's death should be kept a secret, just as his fathers had been, and Northumberland franticly prepared for the change in succession and for Jane to take her place on the throne. Early historians are quick to point out that the Duke of Northumberland faced yet another concern about Edward's body because an autopsy, which would precede the embalming, might confirm the use of poison. Early historians have also suggested that the body placed beneath the altar of the Chapel of Henry VIII in Westminster Abbey is not Edwards but in fact a young boy who looked similar to him. There is no known evidence that substantiates that claim and without a statement by someone that was present at Edward's death and followed him until his burial, the fate of his body remains a mystery.

Chapter 3. July 1553 – February 1554. Queen Jane, Mary and Wyatt's Rebellion

On 8 July, the Lord Mayor and others were summoned to Greenwich and informed of the King's death and of his will by letters patent; then they were told they should swear to keep it a secret. The following day, Sir John Gates assembled the palace guard and informed them of the King's death and of his will. He also explained that the Lady Mary was not fit to succeed for three reasons: her mother's divorce from Henry VIII, her Catholicism, and her sex. He then ordered them to swear their allegiance to Queen Jane and to the crown of England.

Though great care had been taken to restrict the news to only those directly involved, Mary was at Kenninghall when she heard the news of her brothers' death, possibly from an informant loyal to her. Assuming that she was now to accept the throne as her father had originally indicated in his will, and as yet unaware of any changes, she wrote a letter to the Lords of the Council on 9 July asserting her claim to the crown. She noted how strange it was for them not to have notified her of the tragic news immediately. The Princess was clearly ready to claim the crown and signified that fact to the Lords. The Council quickly responded that she should remain quiet and be an obedient servant to Queen Jane.

That same day the Council, completely subjugated and terrorized by Northumberland, decided to proclaim Lady Jane Queen. Mary Sidney was sent to Jane while she was at Chelsea and the two girls took a water barge to Syon House to wait. Northumberland preceded the Councilors into the room where Mary Sidney and Lady Jane waited. Northumberland then requested that Jane and Mary Sidney proceed with him and the Lords to the Chamber of State, where the bewildered young woman of only 15 years found her parents, husband, mother-in-law, and Lady Northampton, who soon all did her reverence.

Numerous accounts of the following events exist but Peter Heylyn's 1661 *History of the Reformation of the Church of England* used sources slightly under a hundred years old at the time and are likely to be more accurate than many, if not most.

> The Duke of Northumberland informed her that; That the King was dead, and that he had declared her for his next successor in the crown imperial; that this declaration was approved by all the Lords of the Council, most of the peers, and all the judges of the land, which they had testified by the subscription of their names, and all this ratified and confirmed by letters patents, under the great seal of England; that the Lord Mayor, the alderman, and some of the principle citizens had been spoke withal, by whom they were assured of the fidelity of the rest of the city; that there was nothing wanting but her grateful acceptance of the high estate, which God almighty, the sovereign disposer of all crowns, and scepters, (never sufficiently to be thanked by her, for so great a mercy) had advanced her to that therefore she should cheerfully take upon her, the name, title, and estate of Queen of England, France and Ireland, with all the royalties, and preeminence's to the same belonging; receiving at their hands the first fruits of the humble duty (now tendered by them on their knees) which shortly was to be played to her, by the rest of the Kingdom" [Heylyn 159].

Sir Peter reports that after Northumberland's speech, Lady Jane found herself in a great perplexity, not knowing whether to lament the death of the king or to rejoice at her adoption of the kingdom. Heylyn says Jane viewed the crown as a great temptation and took some time in her deliberation. After carefully considering all matters, she tearfully answered:

> "That the laws of the Kingdom, and natural right, standing for the King's sister, she would beware of burthening her weak conscience with a yoke, which did belong to them; that she understood the infamy of those, who had permitted the violation of right to gain a scepter; that it were to mock God, and deride justice, to scruple at the stealing of a shilling, and not at the usurpation of a crown. Besides I am not so young, nor so little read in the guiles of fortune, to suffer my self to be taken by them. If she enrich any, it is but to make them the subject of her spoil, if she raise others, it is but to pleasure herself with their ruins. What she adored yesterday, is today her pastime. And, if I now permit her to adorn, and crown me, I must tomorrow suffer her to crush, and tear me in pieces. Nay with what crown doth she present me. A crown, which hath been violently and shamefully wrestled from Katherine of Aragon; made more unfortunately by the punishment of Ann Boleyn, and others, that wore it after her. And why then would you have me add my blood to theirs, and to be the third victim, from whom this fatal crown may be ravished with the head that wears it? But in case it should not prove fatal unto me, and that all its venom were consumed; if fortune should give me warranties of her constancy: should I be well advised to take upon me these thorns, which would dilacerate, though not kill me outright; to burthen my self with a yoke, which would not fail to torment me, though I were assured not to be strangled with it? My liberty is better, then the chain you proffer me, with what precious stones so ever it be adorned, or of what gold so ever framed. I will not exchange my peace for honorable and precious jealousies, for magnificent and glorious letters. And, if you love me sincerely, and in good earnest, you will rather wish me a secure, and quiet fortune, though mean, then an exalted conditions exposed to the wind, and followed by some dismal fall." [Heylyn 159-160]

Her husband Guildford, who now realized the grandeur of his new position, joined with Jane's parents and challenged her reluctance, but the most persuasive of them was the Duke of Northumberland.

Northumberland again reviewed the will of the late King Edward VI with Jane and she questioned the authenticity of changes made to a will that King Henry VIII had put into place. This aggravated Northumberland and he changed his course of persuasion, but Jane did not yield to his intimidating tactics easily, and only after a long delay she finally conceded. "If what hath been given to me is lawfully mine, may thy Divine Majesty grant me such spirit and grace that I may govern to thy glory and service, to the advantage of this realm." Soon after she was pro-claimed Queen of England with the usual formalities that included sending letters to various statesmen and important bodies within the kingdom formally announcing the new queen and requesting their allegiance. After the formalities of the coro-nation, Jane addressed the current prisoners in the Tower and granted many of them liberty after their years of confinement.

Ambassador M.M. de Courrieres informed the Emperor Charles of Spain that Stephen Gardiner, Bishop of Winchester, Courtenay, and the Duke of Norfolk were to be executed by the new queen on 10 or 11 July. They were told to prepare for their death on 7 July, though this was not, in fact, to occur; Lady Jane felt that it was too heavy of a decision to be made and that she needed to be better established on the throne. They were free to walk within the Tower walls.

Jane Grey was not well known in the kingdom and many held a less-than-favorable opinion of the Duke of Northum-berland, whose overambitious reputation and his manipulation of King Edward VI to alter his father's will and place her on the throne added to the kingdom's lack of enthusiasm. As Jane assumed the role and responsibilities of queen, her time was spent mostly reviewing and signing documents, and unaware of Mary's actions she began to amass loyal supporters in great numbers as she asserted her rightful claim to the throne. As these numbers increased, men also began to join Mary and that now caused concerns within Jane's Council.

By 12 July, it was clear to Northumberland that military operations would be required if he were to defeat the growing army of Mary's and capture the Princess while she was at Ken-ninghall. Northumberland had other problems as well and, though he was certainly the most accomplished military leader of the time, he did not trust the resolution of some of his colleagues and strongly desired to remain in London to protect his interests. The Duke of Suffolk had equal qualifications and could have led the forces, but Queen Jane refused to send her father into battle, fearing being left alone with the Duke, and so the Queen ordered Northumberland to lead the forces himself. "In a few days I will bring the Lady Mary, captive, ordered like a rebel as she is," he said as he departed the Tower. Jane's decision not to send her father proved fatal to Northumberland's plans. The restraint that Northumberland had over the Council while in his presence was now gone and the Lords began to establish who their allies where.

On the morning of 13 July, the Duke of Northumberland departed London. Reports on the size of Northumberland's forces vary from 1,500 to 8,000 foot soldiers, 2,000 soldiers on horses, and a small train of artillery. The Duke of Northumberland reportedly said to Lord Gray of Wilton, who accompanied him as they were riding from London, "Do you see, my Lord, what a conflux of people here is drawn to see us march? And yet of all this multitude, you hear not so much as one that wisheth us success." Meanwhile, Mary moved her growing army from Kenninghall to Framlingham expecting a major battle, because Kenninghall was not easy to defend. The news of the increasing numbers of those supporting Mary arrived at Northumberland's forces, which resulted in a small number of men deserting and a demand for replacements reached the Tower on the night of 15 July.

The Duke of Northumberland reached the outskirts of Cambridge on the morning of 16 July, and as he proceeded toward Bury St. Edmunds, news reached him from Yarmouth of the desertion of eight ships stationed there to seize Princess

Mary if she tied to escape overseas. He was told that the crews had sworn their allegiance to Mary, yet another blow to the Duke's plans.

On 17 July, the Duke of Northumberland retreated from Bury St. Edmunds to Cambridge. There Northumberland had to deal with further desertions from his ranks, coupled with the fact that Mary's forces were continuing to increase, which concerned those still trying to remain loyal to Northumberland's cause. Many of his forces now feared that if Mary took the throne they would be convicted of treason and quickly abandoned Northumberland at the first opportunity. By the time Northumberland had reached Cambridge, he lost about half his forces to desertion but lost none in battle, for no actual battle had occurred.

A letter written the following day reflected the desperation evident among Lady Jane's ever-decreasing circle of followers. The letter bears the Queen's signature and is addressed to Sir John St. Lowe and Sir Anthony Kingstone, Knights, commissioning them to muster forces and march to Buckinghamshire to repress the rebellion as soon as possible. By now, it was rumored that Mary's forces were now estimated to be about 30,000 strong. Jane's Council continued to divide, and a number of Councilors met at the Earl of Pembroke's residence with Pembroke and Arundel in attendance. They denounced Northumberland as a "blood-thirsty tyrant and Mary had the best title to the crown." The Mayor of London requested that if no reply came from the notice sent to the Duke of Northumberland, Arundel would go to Cambridge and arrest the villain who had led so many against Mary.

Mary was proclaimed Queen the same day, and the Council changed its allegiance publicly and officially by sending two of their number to tell Suffolk that Jane's reign was over, informing the foreign Ambassadors that the Lady Mary was Queen, proclaiming Mary in London and the provinces, and sending her their loyal submission. When the Duke of Suffolk learned that his daughter's reign was over he quickly went to her and forbid her further use of any royal ceremonies, then instructed her to be content with her return to private life. She replied calmly:

> Sir, I better brook this message, than my forced advancement to royalty; out of obedience to you and my mother I have grievously sinned, and offered violence to myself: now I do willingly, and as obeying the motions of my soul, relinquish the crown, and endeavor to salve those faults committed by others, if at least so great an error may be salved by a willing relinquishment and ingenuous acknowledgement. [Beer, Riot & Rebellion, 160]

Mary issued several proclamations on 19 July, including one to prevent any controversy in religion and preaching. This was done to prevent problems that would result in the change of religions, as Edward VI and Lady Jane were Protestant and Mary was Catholic. The Queen also issued a proclamation to prevent the printing of anything without a license, one covering the issuance of new money, one to prevent seditious rumors, and finally one announcing her accession. Mary also issued orders that all foreigners in her kingdom, who had fled their countries after committing misdeeds such as murder, treason, robbery, and other horrible crimes, should leave England immediately or face the punishment of imprisonment, confiscation of all their belongings, or death if they did not do so.

The following day, the Duke of Northumberland learned at Cambridge that Mary was proclaimed Queen. At about five o'clock that evening, he proclaimed Mary at the Market-Cross in town by throwing up his cap among others in a token of joy. Within an hour, he received the following letter in the name of Queen Mary, ordering him and his band to disarm:

> Ye shall command and charge in the Queen's Highness's Name, the said Duke to disarm himself, and to cease all his Men of War, and to suffer no Part of his Army to do any Thing contrary to Peace, and himself to forbear Coming to this City, until the Queen's Pleasure be expressly declared

unto him. And if he will shew himself like a good quiet Subject, we shall then continue, as we have begun, as humble Suitors to our Sovereign Lady the Queen's Highness for him, and his, as for ourselves. And if he do not, we will not fail to spend our Lives, in Subduing him and his. Item, ye shall declare the like Matter to the Marquess of Northampton, and all other Noblemen and Gentlemen, and to all Men with any of them. And ye shall, in all Places where you come, notify it, if the Duke of Northumberland do not submit himself to the Queen's Highness, Queen Mary, he shall be accepted as a Traitor. And all we of the Nobility, that were Counsellors to the late King, will, to the uttermost Portion, persecute him, and his, to their utter Confusion.

Signed by *Thomas* Archbishop of *Canterbury*, *Thomas* Bishop of *Ely*, Chancellor; *William* Marquess of *Winchester*, Treasurer; *Henry* Duke of *Suffolk*; the Earls of *Bedford*, *Shrewsbury*, and *Pembroke*; *Thomas Darcy* Lord Chamberlain, *W. Peter* Secretary, *W. Cecil* 2nd Secretary, with others of the Council. [Collins 24]

Perhaps in response to a request from the Marchioness of Exeter or from her Councilor, Mary agreed to release Courtenay on 22 July after fifteen years of confinement in the Tower. The Bishop of Winchester and the Duke of Norfolk did not receive their liberty but it was expected that the Queen would do so soon. The Spanish Ambassadors in England wrote to the Emperor on 23 July informing him of the events in England. In their first description of Courtenay, they praised him and described how he had turned his time in confinement into many virtuous and praiseworthy studies, with his indulgence in letter writing displaying his proficiency of the languages, his study of science, and proficiency with several musical instruments. "There is in him a civility which must be deemed natural rather than acquired by habit of society," one Ambassador mentions. They continue in their praise by stating, "His bodily graces are in proportion to those of his mind."

The Spanish Ambassadors described the celebrations going on in London to the Emperor. A bell tower that was modified to hold artillery was rung for two days. The people had great bonfires that could be see for miles, held public banquets in the streets, and there was even some handing out of small amounts of money as everyone showed how happy they were with the rightful heir on the throne.

By 23 July, most gentlemen of rank desired time with the Queen to pay her tribute and to request her forgiveness for their actions in supporting Jane while she was Queen. Mary forgave the majority of them. Questions soon began to circulate in Court as to whom the Queen would marry. Few believed that she would attempt to govern the realm without the guidance of a husband and the name Edward Courtenay was mentioned several times; it was suggested that it was Mary's destiny to marry Courtenay.

Rumors also circulated that the Queen would marry Cardinal Pole. Though not actually ordained, his religious views pleased the Queen and she had a high regard for the man. With Courtenay's apparent lack of interest in marrying the Queen, it was considered that Cardinal Pole would marry the Queen because he possessed the qualities of a mature nature and royal blood, and the union would be considered acceptable in the kingdom. Though the Cardinal had been tried for treason and banned from England during the reign of Henry VIII, his religious views were the same as the Queen's, which made him a strong ally with the Church. Honored by the consideration given him, he declined, due in part to his age; at the time he was 53 years old (Mary was 37).

The Duke of Northumberland and his party surrendered at Cambridge to the Earl of Arundel on 24 July. They reached London the following day at dusk to find large crowds lining the streets and the guards escorting the Duke dealt severely with a mob that threw stones, rotten eggs, and filth from the gutters at the Duke. One witness says that a dead cat was hurled at him. The mob attempted to rush the Duke, shouting, "Death! Death to the traitor!" The once confident, powerful, and arrogant Duke of

Northumberland tried to hold his head up but the humiliation was too much and a witness noticed tears flowing down his face. The Duke of Northumberland was confined to the Tower with his eldest son, the Earl of Warwick, two of his younger sons, Lord Ambrose and Lord Henry Dudley, his brother Sir Andrew Dudley, the Marquess of Northampton, the Earl of Huntingdon, Sir Thomas Palmer, and Sir John Gates. The following day the Duke of Suffolk, among others, joined the growing list of prisoners in the Tower. Jane and Guildford where brought in with the Duchess of Northumberland on 23 or 24 July. Suffolk, though at first arrested, appears to have gained his freedom about 31 July with the understanding that he would surrender himself if required to do so at any time.

Many important letters that the French sent to various locations (such as Scotland) that crossed England were written in code to prevent or at least make it difficult for others to read without a key. Two such letters were intercepted from the Ambassador de Noailles addressed to the French King, and de Noailles indicated that they were taken from him around 1 August. Simon Renard, Ambassador in England at the time, and Royall Tyler, editor of a collection of translated letters from the period, were both unable to decipher one of the two letters. Without the key, the contents of the letter will most likely continue to be unknown.

On 2 August, Mary responded to the numerous inquisitions and suggestions regarding her marriage by various individuals, including some members of her Council, by declaring that she had not considered the thought of marriage while a private citizen but preferred to end her days in chastity. Furthermore, as she now occupied a public position, the Emperor, whom she apparently regarded as a father, guided her and who suggested that she should consider the idea of marriage. Mary indicated that she would choose whomever he had suggested but would not come to a decision without seeing and hearing him first. Mary continued to consider Courtenay a worthy suitor. Born into a noble family that often married into royalty, the name of Courtenay was well known, respected, and trusted in the kingdom and would most certainly be an acceptable union.

Queen Mary reviewed the remaining prisoners in the Tower on 3 August, including the Duke of Norfolk, Gardiner, Tonstal, and Bonner, who where originally confined because of their stubborn adherence to the Catholic religion, and pardoned them. The Duke of Norfolk's attainment was made null and invalid and all were given their liberty. The Queen then restored Edward Courtenay to his father's honors, making him the Earl of Devon. Courtenay found it difficult to express his appreciation to the Queen for his release and restoration of his honors after so many years of confinement.

The Emperor received a letter at about this same time that more information regarding the death of Edward VI had become known. A visit by the Duchess of Suffolk to the Queen informed her that the Duke of Northumberland murdered her husband and that Northumberland had poisoned the young King Edward VI. The Ambassadors also mentioned an apothecary who had committed suicide by drowning himself when he learned that the Duke had been captured, possibly to prevent anyone from learning of certain misdeeds.

As several weeks passed, Courtenay continued to dismiss all notions of entering into marriage with Mary, though cautiously — because if he offended her, his return to the Tower would certainly be imminent. Mary was used to having her way as a princess and now even more so as Queen, and she became frustrated with Courtenay's apparent lack of cooperation.

Enjoying his freedom, Courtenay began to discover the world outside the Tower walls and on 13 August he and his mother attended a service in the church of St. Paul. While listening to the sermon delivered by Dr. Bourne, several individuals began an uproar. They insulted the preacher when he mentioned that the Bishop of London, who was present, and who had been unjustly detained in prison for the past four years because of a sermon he had preached from the same pulpit. Several began to cry aloud, "Papist!" and prevented him from continuing with his sermon. A man pulled out either a small sword or a dagger and threw it at the preacher, trying to kill him, but several members of the congregation prevented him from doing further harm. The Mayor had arrived to lend assistance as Courtenay and his mother succeeded in quieting down the crowd and possibly preventing a small riot. It was overheard afterward that if it were intended they should change their religion, it would be better to set the Duke of Northumberland free. The following week several members of the Council and the yeoman of the guard were present for the protection of the preacher at St. Paul's.

It is also at about this point in time that a historian indicated that Courtenay was seen with several prostitutes and visited several brothels, which agitated the Queen. However, it seems illogical that someone with Courtenay's social status and with the availability of ladies in and around Court he would frequent those establishments, especially after having been considered as a worthy suitor for the Queen.

The Spanish Ambassadors in England had expressed their concern to the Emperor in a letter of 16 August about the Lady Elizabeth. They were apprehensive that she might "conceive some dangerous design," either by her own ambition or perhaps persuaded by someone, and would be difficult to prevent her from doing so because she was "clever and sly." Meanwhile, Mary began to deal with those who opposed her succession to the crown. Members of the kingdom and even Mary herself enthusiastically the followed trial and resulting punishment of at least one culprit, the tyrannical Duke of Northumberland, whose struggle for power had claimed many innocent lives. In what is described as a very colorful trial, the Duke was convicted of high treason and sentenced to death. Before his execution took place, Northumberland announced his conversion to Catholicism, most likely in an attempt to receive mercy from Mary. On 23 August on the Tower Hill the Duke of Northumberland was executed by a lame headsman who "competently dispatched" him with a single blow before a large crowd eager to see the fate of the man that so many loathed. Sir Thomas Palmer and Sir John Gates followed soon after. The Duke of Northumberland was then buried in the chapel of St. Peter-ad-Vincula above Anne Boleyn and Katherine Howard and next to the man he had helped to destroy (by playing a vital role in his trial and execution), Somerset.

The Ambassadors of the Emperor Charles V King of Spain (Philip's father), who where in England, wrote to the Emperor on 27 August updating him with the current events in the kingdom. The Ambassadors included information that the Earl of Pembroke had given Courtenay several presents of a sword and poniard, a basin and ewer, and several horses worth more than three thousand crowns. It has been suggested that Pembroke gave these gifts to Courtenay hoping that Courtenay, who was now in great favor with the Queen, would use his influence with her so Pembroke could get a seat on the Council. In the same letter, the Ambassadors also commented on the state of the Council. They stated that it was their opinion that the Council was not composed of experienced men endowed with the necessary qualities to conduct the administration and government of the kingdom, and several were more inclined towards greed than what they would deem acceptable. The fact that they rarely agreed with one another on matters was a cause of concern.

On the same day, the French Ambassador M. de Gye delivered letters from the King of France that were addressed to Courtenay, who in turn quickly sent them to his mother, who would deliver their contents to the Queen hoping to prevent any suspicion. That same day, the French Ambassadors feasted with several members of the Council, including Courtenay, who they believed to be a member of the Council, with the intent to make his acquaintance without arousing suspicions. The Spanish Ambassadors quickly addressed their concerns to the Queen regarding these letters addressed to Courtenay, indicating that it was strange and intolerable behavior for someone like Courtenay to receive letters of these types and that it was their opinion that it was done to give Courtenay credit and a taste of what it feels like to rule. In response to the contents of the letters, the Ambassadors also mentioned that if a marriage of Courtenay and Elizabeth were allowed, it would be dangerous to Mary because both already had a following and the French had taken notice of this. Though only a few had talked about the possibility of Courtenay marrying the Lady Elizabeth, the content of and suggestions in the letters brought the issue forward and would continue to be a topic of discussion for a long period of time.

The French Ambassadors had reported to the Spanish Ambassadors in England that the French King had discussed the marriage between the Queen and Emmanuel Philibert, Prince of Piedmont (Italy), who would become the Duke of Savoy on his father's death. The Spanish Ambassadors reported on the same date of 27 August that news had arrived that Prince Philip of Spain was soon to depart to Seville for the celebration of his marriage with the Infanta of Portugal.

The Queen, now firmly on the throne, addressed another issue, though less mainstream, to reform the coinage because those now in circulation were made of a poor alloy and there was a great deal of confusion regarding the rate of exchange for foreign coins. On 3 September 1553, a Charter of Creation was written for Edward Courtenay to be the Earl of Devon, with the remainder of his estates upon his death to go to his male heirs and a grant for the better maintenance of his estate with an annuity of 20l from the Petty Customs in the Port of London.

Mary began to put her kingdom in order and among the changes that were taking place was religion. It was no secret that Mary and her sister Elizabeth had conflicting religious views. Mary had attempted to convert Elizabeth to Catholicism but she would not do so and this began to strain their relationship. During the first weeks that Mary was Queen, Elizabeth accompanied her sister in most of the ceremonies, but as time went on Elizabeth was seen less and less as the date of Mary's coronation grew closer.

It was suggested that in the next session of Parliament that the marriage between Henry VIII and Catherine would be deemed lawful, thus annulling the former act of Parliament that declared Mary a bastard. The reason for this was that the previous act declared the marriage between Anne Boleyn and Henry to be legal (thus legitimizing Elizabeth) and alleviated any concerns that Princess Elizabeth or others may have had.

On 27 September, Mary traveled to the Tower by river with her sister Elizabeth and other ladies, where they were greeted by a great display of guns upon their arrival as preparations for her coronation moved into the final phases. On 29 September, the Queen created fifteen knights of the bath, who were knighted by the Earl of Arundel, whom the Queen had appointed as her great master of the household. Under a tradition that dates to about

AD 1127, special knighthood was given on important royal occasions such as coronations. The name "knights of the bath" derives from the ancient ceremony wherein individuals participated in a vigil of fasting, prayer, and bathing on the day before being knighted. Among these new knights were Edward Courtenay, Earl of Devon; Thomas, Earl of Surry; Lord William Herbert of Cardiff; Lord Henry Abergavenny; Lord John Lumley; Lord James Montjoy; Sir Henry Jerningham; Sir William Powlett; Sir Henry Clinton; Sir Hugh Rich; Sir Henry Paget; Sir Henry Parker; and Sir William Dormer.

On 30 September, the Queen rode through the city of London towards Westminster, riding in a chariot of cloth tissue that was drawn by six horses adorned with similar tissue. Mary wore a lavish gown of purple velvet draped with powdered furs of ermine. On her head, she wore a ball of cloth of tinsel inset with pearl and a lavish stone, and above that was a round circle of gold that was richly adorned with precious jewels. This headdress was so large that Mary had to support her head with her hand and the canopy was raised to accommodate the headdress. Ahead of Mary's chariot rode several gentlemen and knights, then the doctors of divinity, bishops, Lords, members of the Council, and the knights of the bath in their robes. Courtenay's location is uncertain; he may have ridden in the front ranks with other gentlemen or perhaps with the Knights of the Bath, as he had just been made a member and was certainly proud of displaying such. Following the knights of the bath were the Bishop of Winchester, the Marquess of Winchester, Lord High Treasurer, and the Earl of Oxford, who carried a sword, just ahead of Mary. The Mayor of London wore a gown of crimson velvet and carried the scepter of gold.

Next was the Queen's chariot led by Sir Edward Hastings holding the horse's reins with his hands. Following the Queen was another chariot covered in cloth of silver and white, and the horses were draped with similar cloth. This chariot carried the Lady Elizabeth and the Lady Anne of Cleves. Following Elizabeth's chariot was a long train of 46 ladies and gentlewomen wearing gowns of red velvet and riding horses draped with the same. Several pageants followed the procession in different locations.

Mary was crowned the following day, 1 October 1553, by the Bishop of Winchester in the magnificently adorned Westminster Abbey. Courtenay carried a sword during the precession, as did the Earl of Westmoreland, and the Earl of Shrewsbury carried the crown. The Duke of Norfolk served as Marshal and the Earl of Arundel was Lord Steward. Following the oath of allegiance and ceremonies was a lavish feast, were Mary was offered 312 dishes. Over seven thousand dishes were offered to all those in attendance, of which 4900 were declared waste and offered to the poor citizens following the banquet.

On 2 October 1553, Cardinal Pole, while in Trent, wrote a long letter to Courtenay.

Cardinal Pole to Edward Courtenay, Marquess of Exeter:

The greater the joy felt by Pole internally for his cousin's release from distress and imprisonment, and for the recovery of his state and property, the less able is he to express it externally by words to his satisfaction, though his love for Courtenay will not allow him to omit demonstrating it as he best may by letter; nor can his congratulations on Courtenay's individual good fortune be complete, unless they include those for the common weal, which God has granted to England, and on which Courtenay's personal welfare depends; in like manner as not one can rejoice at any good fruit without rejoicing at the tree which produced it, and also with the planter of that tree. In the present case, the tree is the goodness of the Queen, who has been placed on the throne by the miraculous hand of God, for the consolation of all lovers of virtue and piety, and most especially of those who have suffered on that account. That the Queen by this first fruit of her justice should have relieved Courtenay from such unjust oppression, cannot but give great pleasure to all those who see hand hear for it; above all, because he is the flower of the ancient nobility of England which its adversaries sought especially to destroy root and branch. This is the first joy felt by Pole at so gracious an act performed by the Queen, and it is common to many others; but Pole's personal joy proceeds from the singular love which be bears Courtenay, not solely from the natural ties of kindred, but by reason of the affection and love which Courtenay's most illustrious father always evinced both towards Pole and his brother; and the late Marquess of Execter and Lord Montacute having been so linked by God in sincere affection throughout their lives, he would not at the last hour allow them to be separated, both dying together for the same cause on Tower Hill, 9 January 1539, which was that of god, the most noble and glorious of any.

But to return to what was said about the love of Courtenay's father for Pole, he mentions the following pledge (*pegno*). On Pole's last departure from England [for Avignon, in 1531], he was the last English nobleman with whom Pole spoke, being invited to go and see him, as he was then sick; and the first words uttered to him by the Marquess were, "Lord Cousin Pole, your departure from the realm at this present time, shows in what a miserable state we find ourselves. It is to the universal shame of all us nobles, who allow you to absent yourself, when we ought most to avail ourselves of your presence; but being unable to find any other remedy for this, we pray God to find it himself." These were the last words he ever said to Pole, which, proceeding as they did from the cordial love he bore him, Pole has always treasured in his heart; and this causes him to rejoice at all the good fortune of England, most especially as it shows yet more clearly that the remedy for which he said they must pray to God has already arrived, in such a form that the whole world can see that it proceeded solely from Divine providence, which ordained that as the misery of that period, and all that ensued subsequently, came through a woman, so should reparation come through a virgin, their gracious Queen.

Courtenay will thus clearly know the double cause which Pole has for joy and comfort at all Courtenay's prosperity; and the third cause of his rejoicing, and which confirms both the others is, that he hears from many persons who know Courtenay, and are of sound judgment, that during the whole period of his tribulation, although under bodily imprisonment, and utterly deprived of his revenue, all his estates being confiscated, yet did he nevertheless comfort himself in such a way, that so far as his tender age in so hard a case could demonstrate, it was clearly manifest that the nobility of his mind and imitation of his father's virtues, the greatest inheritance that a father can leave his son, were never imprisoned for taken from honour; and seeing him already arrived at years of discretion, and by Providence of God, and by means of her most gracious Majesty, set at liberty, they firmly hope also to see and enjoy the mature fruits of his virtue in all things relating to the honour of God, and of his Holy Church, for the consolation in the first place of his mistress supreme (vostra suprema signora), and secondly, of all the friends of his true honour and prosperity, amongst whom Pole considers himself one who does not give way to any other. In conclusion, recommends himself to his mot illustrious cousin and Lord until such time as it shall please God to make the road for him, and open the door, so that he may personally congratulate Courtenay, whom he requests to perform the like due office in Pole's name, cordially and affectionately, with the most illustrious mother.

Is writing this letter on his way to Germany, towards the Court of the Emperor, to whom and to the King of France conjointly he has been sent as Legate by the Pope, to treat the peace between them. Hopes the Almighty will vouchsafe to grant it, for the consolation and benefit of all Christendom.

From Trent, 2nd October 1553. [State Papers, Venice 423]

The Cardinal's praise for the Queen releasing Courtenay is evident in the letter. Interestingly the letter mentions both the Cardinal and Courtenay in the third person; this is perhaps a result of the translation of the letter from Italian to English. It has been suggested that the Cardinal had written in the expectation that Courtenay may become his sovereign and did so to remain in his favor.

Apparently Courtenay had maintained certain animosities towards the Cardinal's brother, for in a letter from the Emperor to the Ambassador Simon Renard dated 8 October, the Emperor had made mention of an "exhibition made by Courtenay against Cardinal Pole's brother." There is no additional information. In another letter from the Emperor to Don Juan Manrique de Lara, the Imperial Ambassador in Rome, dated 11 October, the Emperor mentions that when the Cardinal's brother Geoffrey Pole had returned to England from Liege, Courtenay had made a treat to kill him, asserting that the Cardinal's father had been the cause of his father's death. If Courtenay had any animosities toward either the Cardinal or his brother, the Cardinal did not reflect on them in his letter of 2 October.

The Spanish Ambassadors wrote to the Emperor informing him of the Queen's coronation and that Adrian Crole was waiting on his orders, as the French had indicated that they would retake the islands of Sark and Guernsy, which lie between England and France, at any cost. Crole requested additional garrisons on the small islands because the sailors there were dissatisfied with their rations, disorderly, and complained that with no proper means to store the beer that it must be drank immediately.

Mary's consideration for Courtenay as a husband had now diminished, though he continued to reject all advances made on the Queen's behalf in a way that was as polite as possible, despite the report from an advisor that observations were made of Courtenay and Elizabeth spending more time together than usual. It is perhaps this report that laid the foundation for further controversy regarding a possible union between Courtenay and Princess Elizabeth.

Mary was faced with ever-increasing debts and less available funds to pay them because of the numerous military campaigns that were currently ongoing and those of recent past that contributed to depleting her funds. This prompted the Queen to look for money outside the kingdom, and she was soon advised that Prince Philip of Spain would serve the needs of both the kingdom and the Queen, as her husband. Courtenay, though of noble blood and a worthy match, could not assist with the ever-increasing royal debts. It was about this point that Protestants began to leave England, fearful of Mary having now restored the Catholic religion to the kingdom as she began her cruel persecution by executing a few Bishops and others because of their obstinacy. There had been further discussion about bringing the Cardinal back to England, but with the current conditions, the Council felt that he could now be the pretext for attacks on religion which would be hard to guard against and that he best stay where he was. At about this same time, two servants of Courtenay had reported to him about two plots they had overheard regarding a man named St. Leger who was about to leave for Ireland with the pay for the troops. They stated that three English captains who would accompany him had been bribed to seize the money and kill all those who were not in the plot, then leave for Scotland or France. Courtenay's report had most likely saved the lives of those men and the pay for the troops was dispatched in secret.

By mid-October, Mary's interest in marrying Courtenay had changed to marrying Prince Philip of Spain. On 23 October, Simon Renard wrote to the Emperor to inform him of certain situations in England, and he reported that the Queen had met with the Bishop of Winchester, the Controller, Walgrave, Inglefield, and Southwell, who encouraged the Queen to marry Courtenay because the kingdom would never support a foreigner and Courtenay was the only possible match for her. Mary had told them to weigh the current state of affairs in the kingdom, such as the French plotting and the marriage of the French Dauphin with the Queen of Scotland, and what benefit the kingdom could look for if she were to marry Courtenay and what profit might accrue to it if she chose a foreigner. The Queen continued that she had "no liking for Courtenay" and had not completely made her mind up regarding the matter. Mary mentioned that she had heard that the French would do as much as possible to prevent the marriage of Philip and Mary. The Queen then suggested that Simon Renard request the conditions of an alliance with Philip to the Emperor and send them to her so that she could review them in private; Renard replied that he would do so. At this point, it was clear to most who Mary's choice was, and it was not popular.

At about the same time, a session of Parliament had concluded and among the Acts that passed were the restoration of Edward Courtenay and his mother to their previous honors and the declaration that the sentence, imprisonment, and execution of their respective father and husband should imply no disgrace to them. Soon after, news arrived in the Court that the French Ambassador was doing everything he could do to win over

Courtenay. Princess Elizabeth was forced to deal with the constant talk of her marriage to Courtenay, but was afraid to discuss the matter with him except with witnesses present to avoid fueling the suspicions that were already present. The Queen was greatly concerned with a two-hour meeting that took place between the French Ambassador and Elizabeth, and members of the Council had heard news of plotting. No record exists of the actual conversation, but it was clear that the French supported the marriage of Courtenay to Elizabeth and would even show their support in the form of money, which was later revealed. By now, Mary had decided that an alliance with Prince Philip would be in the best interest of her kingdom. Simon Renard wrote to the Emperor on 31 October, again requesting the conditions of an alliance that Mary had previously asked for. Renard recommended to the Queen and the Emperor that Courtenay should now marry Princess Elizabeth based on the opinions of several members of the Council.

The marriage of the Queen of England with a foreigner was not popular with the few that knew of it, including Courtenay, and it has been suggested that he did in fact address the Queen on the matter. These actions increased the suspicions about him and on the same day, Mary opened and read several letters addressed to Courtenay written by Pole while he was at Innsbruck. The letters only mentioned the legation to Philip and the King of France, and requested that Courtenay be a faithful subject and show his gratitude for the benefits he had received from the Queen. That evening of the same day, the Queen requested that Renard meet her, and together they met with Mrs. Clarence and discussed the letter she had received from the Emperor. The letter, she said, had caused her sleeplessness and she had continually wept and prayed to God to give her the guidance she needed to arrive at a decision regarding the questions of marriage that Renard first raised while at New Hall. Renard informed the Queen that Prince Philip possessed numerous virtuous qualities, would be a good husband to her, and would do all that he could help her with all the affairs of the kingdom. The Queen pretended to be sick for a couple of days so she could think about the proposal without any unnecessary disturbances or distractions. Mary had a plethora of concerns regarding such an alliance, but it would appear by the way history has recorded the events that she was thinking of the well being of the kingdom above all.

Courtenay's reactions regarding Mary's choice for a husband is clear in a letter that Renard wrote to the Emperor dated 4 November. The letter mentioned that Courtenay had reacted quickly to Mary's letters of confirmation from Philip by attempting to win over several gentlemen, including the Chancellor Stephen Gardiner, who were close to Mary in an attempt to prevent the negotiations for the marriage from continuing. Courtenay had also visited the sick Inglefield three times, hoping that he would go to Mary's court and represent his interests. He also sought advice from the Earl of Pembroke twice. In a prudent decision, the Chancellor who represented the interest of several individuals decided to approach Parliament and have them address the issue with the Queen regarding the unpopular decision that she has made, fearing that if they carried it any further on their own, their actions could constitute an act of treason. The Chancellor had based his arguments against the match on two sets of assertions. First was that, if the marriage took place, England would go to war with France and cause the country to suffer. This would be coupled with the King of Bohemia plotting in Germany to prevent Philip's succession, and the Italian Princes would join forces with the French to prevent it. The second reason is that the English people and nobility would never tolerate the Spaniards in their country, as they regarded the Spanish as being proud and impertinent.

Renard attempted to describe the emotions that many were apparently feeling, including Courtenay himself, in a letter to the Emperor. "In the streets one sees nothing but Courtenay displaying the jealousy felt by rivals in love, and all believe he is jealous of the crown rather than of its wearer." Renard claims at this point that both the French and Venetian Ambassadors were proceeding with greater care than before since receiving information from Courtenay or his ministers that the Queen was informed of their communications with him and that the King of France had promised Courtenay so much that he may be satisfied with just half. It appeared that Mary could trust fewer and fewer people and her reactions were purely defensive as she restricted those with access to her and would address the Chancellor in a private meetings to prevent the matter from continuing by reminding him of the oath she swore to at her coronation and of her duty to the crown. Mary had hoped the same approach would prevent the Earl of Pembroke from continuing to support Courtenay also.

On 13 November, Lady Jane and her husband Guildford were brought to trial. Unfortunately, no actual transcript has survived about the trial of Lady Jane other than the notes indexed in the Additional Manuscript collection (article 10617) currently housed in the British Library. Very few accounts remain of the actual trial, with the following as the most vivid of them:

> Lady Jane appeared before her judges in all her wonted loveliness: her fortitude and composer never forsook her; nor did the throng and bustle of the Court, the awful appearance of the seat of judgment, or the passing of the solemn sentence of the law, seem to disturb her mind: of their native bloom her cheeks were never robbed, nor did her voice seem once to falter: on the beauteous traitress every eye was fixed; and the grief that

reigned throughout the whole assembly bespoke a general interest in her fate: indeed,

> "Her very judges wrung their hands for pity:
> Their old hearts melted in 'em as she spoke,
> And tears ran down upon their silver beards.
> E'en her enemies were moved, and for a moment
> Felt wrath suspended in their doubtful breasts,
> And questioned if the voice they heard were mortal." [Bayley 428]

Lady Jane and Guildford were found guilty of treason and sentenced to death, though at the time they believed Queen Mary would forgive them and release them to lead a private life after serving some length of imprisonment. On the same day, the Archbishop Cranmer and the Lords Ambrose and Henry Dudley were taken from the Tower under guard with an estimate of four hundred men and arraigned for high treason at the Guild-hall "for having levied war against the Queen, and conspired to set up another in her room." They all pleaded guilty, and the sentence that was passed on them was subsequently confirmed by attainder in Parliament.

The following day the Queen informed Simon Renard that Courtenay's mother had requested a visit with her to request leave for her son to dine with the Venetian Ambassadors on the Thursday last. The Queen sharply responded that he had done so often without requesting leave before and that she hoped that he would behave in all respects and do nothing inconsistent with his duty. It was about this time that problems began for Princess Elizabeth. There had always been a certain amount of animosity between Mary and Elizabeth, and the rumors of the possible uprisings and placing Elizabeth and Courtenay on the throne only aggravated the already strained relationship. As a result, Elizabeth and Courtenay were now more closely watched, with reports of their activities given to the Queen.

Three days later, on 17 November, Lady Jane Grey's father, the Duke of Suffolk, had "made his confession as to religion," and the Queen remitted his fine and reinstated him by means of a general pardon. The Queen had also pardoned the Earl of Huntingdon, because both men had declared their undying loyalty and would support the Queen regardless of her choice of a husband. Though Queen Mary had received numerous descriptions of her husband to be, she had not yet seen a portrait of him and requested that Renard locate one. Renard did in fact locate a three-year old portrait that had been painted by Titan and was in the possession of the Queen Dowager, who in turn informed Renard in her letter of 19 November that it was being sent to the Queen. The Queen Dowager indicated that the painting had suffered a little from time and that it should be viewed in proper light, looked at from a distance, and realized that the likeness was not exact.

A couple of days later, Simon Renard wrote to the Emperor with several updates on events in the kingdom. Renard had told the Emperor that Paget had received word that Courtenay had wished him ill health, and according to a letter from the Ambassador de Noailles to the King of France, Courtenay had plotted to have Paget and Arundel murdered. Then he would flee the country because he seemed to favor the foreigners. Renard recommended that care should be taken towards the brother of Walgrave, who had left the country and returned to the service of the Queen Dowager of Hungary because he was a loyal supporter of Courtenay. Renard concluded the letter with a recount of his dinner at the house of the Earl of Bedford, Lord Privy Seal, with most of the Council and Courtenay present, who had "behaved in a way that showed his dislike towards him in what he indicated as a very violent manner."

It was about this point in time that rumors had leaked out to the common people that Mary had now indicated her choice for a husband was no longer Courtenay but Prince Phillip of Spain. This was not a popular choice with the commoners, as many remembered that the Spanish/English history was often bloody and many feared that England would be invaded because of this alliance. This news prompted some to action, revealed in later court proceedings, it was indicated that William Pickering and others met in the Parish of St. Gregory in Castell Baynerde ward London on 23 November with Thomas Wyatt and George Harper to discuss the removal of Mary from the throne. They planned to marry Elizabeth and Edward Courtenay and place them on the throne in her place. The rising was set to take place on 18 March 1554.

There are some suggestions that Edward Courtenay first formed these groups, but it was Thomas Wyatt, son of the well-known poet the elder Thomas Wyatt, that history has most often regarded as the leader. Among the main instigators involved with Wyatt was Henry Grey, the Duke of Suffolk (Jane's father), two of his brothers, Peter Carew, and Nicholas Throckmorton. Several theories exist concerning what the conspirators had hoped to procure. Among them was Mary's removal, thus preventing the marriage, and restoring Lady Jane to the throne. Another was Edward Courtenay's marriage to Princess Elizabeth to place them on the throne. No real physical evidence exists supporting either of these theories, and they may continue to remain conjecture unless some obscure document surfaces proving either theory as fact.

The marriage was only one of reasons that motivated the risings, and is a little more complex than is often portrayed. Those that followed Wyatt did so for a variety of reasons. Some, including Wyatt himself, feared a Spanish takeover of their government and the great sums of English money that would be spent on Spanish interests not relevant to English affairs. Others were diehard Protestant, and with Mary a devoted and stanch Catholic, her marriage to another Catholic was like adding salt to a wound. Yet others may have seen Wyatt as an instrument for expressing unresolved grievances, while some followed as a result of peer pressure or influenced by friends, family, their employers, or landlords.

Whatever may be interpreted some 450 years after the risings, there was nevertheless a treaty drawn to cover all the issues and concerns of the realm. The drafts began late in November and were completed in late December 1553 and early January of 1554. The treaty included provisions that Phillip would enjoy the title of King, but the real power over the realms and kingdom would belong to Mary only. If she were to die without an heir, Phillip would have no claim to the throne, but, if the union produced a son, then the son would have all rights. Phillip's obligations with Spain would not change, but the two realms would not converge in political matters and Phillip would obey all English laws and customs. Regardless of the treaty, the conspirators continued with their plans, and news of this began to flow to the far outskirts of the kingdom and beyond. As ten-sions grew, Renard wrote to the Emperor mentioning that the French Ambassador had said in the presence of a full Council that the French had sunk a large number of Spanish ships, with the damages at about six or seven million in gold.

In the first week of December, the Queen quickly responded to rumors that Elizabeth was lending an ear to certain French heretics by questioning the Princess of these activities, of which she denied any knowledge. In a letter from Ambassador Noailles to the King of France, he states that Elizabeth would gladly wed Courtenay and go with him to the West Country to try to head a rebellion, but that Courtenay had been intimidated. Attempting to distance herself from the scandals, and by now tired of the interrogations, Princess Elizabeth courteously took leave of the Queen on December 7 to stay at her childhood home in Ashridge, departing on the same road along which the French Ambassadors had petitioned to have posting-houses. Prior to her departure, she was questioned again, but this time by Arundel and Paget, who had told her that they were suspicions of her actions. The Princess did everything in her power to try to alleviate any concerns that the Queen had and denied any such rumors were true, but this would never be, as the Queen would always remain suspicious of her sister's activities. Following that interview, the Queen met with Courtenay in the presence of his mother and Paget, and after a long series of questions she was satisfied with the answers that Courtenay had given, at least for the time being, though both he and Elizabeth would be continually watched.

On 15 December 1553, the Chiefs of Ten wrote a letter to Giacomo Soranzo, Venetian Ambassador in England:

> Are certain that by their letter of the 25th ult. About his withdrawing adroitly from the matter of religion in England, he will of his prudence have also understood their intention with regard to other negotiations about matter unconnected with the Signory; having nevertheless heard it reported in certain quarters that an envoy (un homo, Renard?) has been sent to England by the most Christian King to persuade Edward Courtenay (al Sig. Cortoni) not to brook the introduction of a foreign King not to wrong himself, the envoy promising him his most Christian Majesty's assistance, and employing his (Soranzo's) mediation with Courtenay; although they do not believe the matter to have passed thus, or that he (Soranzo) meddled with it; will acquaint him with what has been told them, in order that should these suspicions proceed from any close and constant intercourse between and Courtenay, or from other causes of which he will be able to judge, this warning may put him on his guard, so as by Courtesy and address to prevent anyone from suspecting such a thing for the future on such occasions as may hereafter present themselves; and in this the Chiefs are sure he will succeed, by means of his prudence and dexterity.

> Ayes, 28 Noes, 0 Neutrals, 0 [State Papers, Venice, pg. 448]

The letter certainly suggests that rumors of a possible insurrection regarding the marriage of Mary to Phillip made it as far as the Chiefs of Ten in Italy, but more intriguing is that the Chiefs for some reason either knew of or hinted at the possibility of Courtenay's involvement in the insurrection based most likely on information they received. This source may or may not have been totally accurate.

Renard had again presented the idea of the marriage of Courtenay and Elizabeth to the Queen, but as of 17 December, she had still given no answer. He had persuaded her with the fact that the marriage would please the nobility and even went so far as to say that he was told that if the marriage did take place that all the nobility and people of the kingdom would accept and support the marriage of the Queen to a foreign prince. Renard informed the Queen of Elizabeth's request for her opinion on the matter, and said that the Princess had promised Courtenay that she would not speak of the marriage to him or force him to accept it because she had desired to hear from the Queen before making a decision. It would be safe to assume at this point that Elizabeth would have married Courtenay if it was for the good of the kingdom and if the Queen had desired it. But if they did marry, it would seem to have only satisfied a few and only temporarily satisfied those who were upset with the English/Spanish alliance, but their marriage could give additional time that would have been beneficial to the Queen to more effectively deal with the situation.

Elizabeth had written to the Queen with a couple of requests to borrow a litter and ornaments for her chapel, and the Queen granted these requests and ordered them to her at once. On the same day, news arrived to Renard that the French were preparing twenty-four warships and that four were already off the English coast. Spies had reported that the King of France would do whatever was necessary to prevent Philip from landing in England and that he intended to use several of these ships to land men in Scotland, for which the Scots were preparing. Philip soon dispatched his ambassadors to England to negotiate the treaty of alliance between England and Spain and regarding his wedding to the Queen. On 18 December, the Queen Dowager wrote a letter to Garcia de Escalante, who was Captain of the eight ships that were to sail to England with Philip. Along with certain instructions, she warned that the French had stationed warships in the channel between Calais and Dover, and though the eight ships were well equipped with artillery, cannon balls, powder, and men, the need for additional ships was necessary, but none were available at the time and to sail with all caution.

Simon Renard wrote to the Emperor Charles V on 20 December informing him of the events in England. He informed the Emperor that the nobility and people understood that the Council was unanimous in their support of the alliance and that the Earl of Derby had withdrawn his support with Walgrave. Courtenay and the Lord Dacre, Earl of Pembroke, Shrewsbury, and Arundel had assured the Queen of their goodwill and fidelity. Mr. Renard indicated that the contents of the treaty had been revealed and had satisfied all concerns that many had over the alliance. As a result of the treaty, a great deal of the discontent had diminished, and the French and heretics were no longer able to find as many partisans now that there was talk of marrying Courtenay to the Lady Elizabeth. Renard assured the Emperor that many in the kingdom had changed their minds, some out of fear, others out of hope, and still others by reason, hypocrisy, or a desire to please.

With news that Philip had dispatched his ambassadors to England, measures were taken to ensure the security of the border with Scotland. Captains and officers of the seaports were instructed to watch for any hostile ships. The Queen wanted it known to all that she was well armed and ready for anything.

Renard received the Queen's answer regarding the marriage of Courtenay and Elizabeth around 29 December, and she was now completely against the idea of the marriage. Paget disliked it even more because he was told that the nobility no longer desired it. The Chancellor had advised Courtenay to marry another woman in England and not Elizabeth. Renard reported the Queen's answer to the Emperor and said that he had sent spies into France to learn of any activities, but they were simple-minded and did not bring good reports. He would have to look for intelligent people to send who could acquire worthy information. Informants had also passed along information that there were some individuals who were trying to persuade Courtenay to seize the Tower, and Renard advised the Queen to place additional guards there just in case this information was accurate.

On 2 January 1554, the Emperor's ambassadors arrived at the Tower of London and were greeted by many great and noble men who received them displaying all the respect and honor that representatives of the Queen should. At the entrance to the city, Edward Courtenay, the Earl of Devon, greeted them with several other Earls and Lords among a large crowd of people who seemed to be delighted with their arrival. When the Ambassadors enquired when they would see the Queen, they were told that it would be the next day at two o'clock after dinner.

The following day, the same group of English gentlemen conduced the Ambassadors to the Queen, who paid her great respect and formally requested her agreement in the marriage. The remainder of the day was spent reviewing the treaty, which had been drafted and approved by all parties, and addressed several other issues. The Queen was given several letters from Philip, which she read and asked several questions about, including his health and the well-being of several others. The formalities ended with Mary showing the ring on her finger symbolizing her acceptance and trust that Philip meant no harm to the kingdom, still a concern of many. The remainder of their visit was spent in meetings with the Council reviewing the treaty and finally signing it, which put it into effect. Following the formalities, the Ambassadors were entertained in Court activities such as game playing and hunting, and were well cared for, unaware that several of the English gentlemen attending these lavish activities were conspiring to destroy the very thing they were there to secure. The Queen formally announced her marriage to Phillip on 15 January to the public.

It was reported on 7 January that an Italian, Mario Antonio, who was living with Courtenay, discontinued his service with him, perhaps dissatisfied or pretending to be, and was discovered to be plotting against Courtenay on the Scottish border town of Berwick. There is no information as to what Mario was plotting, and the validity of his claims was questionable. It was also discovered that the French were opening all correspondence from England to look for signs of any plotting against the French, and they were preparing ships for battle on the Norman and Breton coasts.

At about this same point in time, January 4th to 6th, news had arrived in Court that Peter Carew, who once held the position of Sheriff of Devon in the thirty-eighth year of the reign of Henry VIII and in the first year of the reign of Edward VI, was raising people in the West and trying to induce Courtenay or the Lady Elizabeth to act as their leader. The Queen quickly responded by sending Carew a summons to appear before the Council immediately. Revealed in later proceedings, Peter Carew approached the Duke of Suffolk and, hoping to secure an alliance with him, told him that if the Queen would forget about marrying a Spaniard and use moderation in all matters of religion that he would be willing to die in her service. Otherwise, he would do the best that he could to place Princess Elizabeth and Courtenay on the throne and he would only be one of a hundred gentlemen that would seize Mary and place her in the Tower.

For reasons that are unclear, Peter Carew began his revolt earlier than was previously agreed. One theory exists that a report was released indicating that Philip was coming before the feast of the purification on 2 February. Another theory suggests that Courtenay had confessed all that he knew about Carew, Wyatt, and the others to Stephen Gardiner prior to the recorded date of the interview of 21 January, which most likely took place sometime between the 8th and 14th of January. Nevertheless, Carew and his followers began the revolt, relying heavily on information that Courtenay would arrive anytime and take command of the forces. He would likely march to meet Suffolk with his forces from the North, and Wyatt with his forces from the East, then they would all march into London with an impressive show of force.

Peter Carew declared war against the Queen while he was at Mountsawtrey on 17 January and made a request for Courtenay to come as quickly as possible into Devonshire, promising that all the inhabitants of the county would support him against the Queen and the Spaniards. Carew had placed horses on the road from London to Devonshire so Courtenay could make his journey as quickly as possible. Then Peter Carew made additional plans in case Courtenay did not arrive in time by informing Gawin Carow and William Gibbes of his plans. They quickly assembled forty men armed with weapons willing to support the cause when they were called upon to begin the revolt.

Courtenay never arrived. The decision not to go must have been a hard one for him to make and someone close to him may have influenced his decision. Regardless, it was perhaps the one decision that would help him to keep his head after the revolt was over. Peter Carew and his followers quickly realized that they were not finding the support they had been promised and hoped for, and without Courtenay's support, Carew chose to flee England to France and possibly secure support there.

On the following day, 18 January 1554, the official entry regarding Courtenay's pardon, though having been pardoned of all crimes almost 5 months ago, was finally recorded on the Pardon Roll of Mary I, along with numerous other gentlemen, citizens, and mercers, as "Edward Courtenay, Knight, Lord Courtney, Earl of Devon." On the same day, Renard dispatched a letter of updates to the Emperor with the news of the rebellions. The Council had declared Peter Carew a traitor and had made several requests for him to appear before them, all of which he disregarded. According to Renard, Courtenay and his followers feared the capture of Carew because of the information that he might divulge upon his capture. Nevertheless, the Council issued orders for his capture and said he was to be placed in the Tower.

The pope had declared his favor for the French and indicated that he would not grant a dispensation for the marriage that the Emperor had requested. Anthony Bonuisi had mentioned to Renard that there were gentlemen in the Emperor's Court who mentioned a promise of marriage that had already been secured between Philip and the Infanta of Portugal. Stephen Gardiner reacted to the Council's request to interrogate Courtenay and to find the limits of his knowledge regarding the risings. There are some indications that suggest that on 21 January, Gardiner questioned Courtenay; how much information he acquired is not known, but it would seem that it was enough to make his position difficult and many concur that at the time he suppressed as much as he could of the interview. Some information was passed to the Council, and others made their own conclusions.

As of 23 January, Peter Carew was still at large and refused to address the Council. In a response to another summons, Carew responded that he did not have any horses to make the long journey to London. The Council then issued another, final summons, and Carew then openly admitted to being a rebel. The Queen responded by sending small garrisons of soldiers, led by the Earl of Pembroke, who would go to the west and Cornwall, the Earl of Shrewsbury, to his county and the Earl of Derby to other counties with full powers to capture him by any means necessary. The Queen by now maintained about seven to eight thousand men to protect her if the need were to arise, not only from the local threats but from the French as well.

Though not actually recorded until mid-February, it was at about this time that Carew had arrived in the French Court and had spoken with the king. Courtenay had also sent a servant to negotiate with the King of France, and after speaking with Carew, the king sent Marshal de St. Andre, Governor of Picardy, who departed at once to take Calais by the request of Courtenay. The Queen's suspicions continued to grow towards Courtenay because he had not visited Court lately and had maintained the company of "ruffians and heretics," and more so now because his mother had became less intimate with the Queen and rarely discussed anything with her.

The Council had devised a plan to test the loyalty of Courtenay by proposing to send him to the Emperor with the pretext of accompanying Thomas Thirlby, Bishop of Norwich, when he would meet with the Emperor to secure his oath on the treaty. They proposed that if Courtenay refused to go, that would be a sign that he was in fact plotting against the marriage, and while he was away whether those devoted to him would continue to be. If Courtenay had refused to go, it would have violated all laws and the Queen could place him in the Tower. That same day, the Chancellor, Renard, and Courtenay met at the Chancellor's house. The Chancellor told Courtenay that he was keeping suspicious company and that it was said by others that he intended to forget his duty towards the Queen. He then told Courtenay that the Queen desired that he go on an honorable mission to meet the Emperor.

Courtenay responded to the Chancellor that although several people had attempted to influence him where religion and the marriage were concerned that he never paid any attention to them, for he had chosen to live and die in the Queen's service. He continued that he had been spoken to about a marriage with the Lady Elizabeth, but he would rather return to the Tower than ally himself to her. As for the mission, he would gladly go, and he felt that it was a great honor for the Queen to consider him for such an assignment. The Chancellor then informed Courtenay that he would find Cardinal Pole currently in Brussels and asked him if he would not like to conduct him to England. Courtenay responded that he would and to defend him against all heretics. When the Queen was informed of the meeting and of Courtenay's responses and conduct, she was pleased, at least for the present.

Renard advised the Emperor of the plan to send Courtenay overseas in a letter that was dispatched on 23 January. It said that the Chancellor had offered him a gentleman who might be sent to Spain through France if the Emperor approved, and that a safe conduct would be demanded for him. If the French refused, the Queen would deny passage by anyone to Scotland.

It was also about this time that Elizabeth wrote to the Queen requesting her forgiveness for not updating the Queen of her activities since she had left Court because she was sick with a cold and had bad headaches. Mary had written several letters to her sister without answer in a short period. In the last letter of that period, Mary told Elizabeth about her decision to marry and of the articles in the treaty. Elizabeth appears to be slightly apprehensive towards the news, but she nevertheless wished the Queen the very best.

For a reason that remains only conjecture, Wyatt chose to proceed with the rebellion earlier than originally planned, and then informed his confidants. It would be safe to speculate that because Carew had "jumped the gun," Wyatt's element of surprise had been compromised and he determined that swift action was his only recourse. Revealed in later trial proceedings, it has been suggested that Sir Nicholas Throgmorton had passed along intelligence to those in the West, and also to Wyatt, that he should begin the revolt and march to London, where he would find the city open and willing to support the cause. He also dispatched a notice to Peter Carew of the same and it has been suggested that Throgmorton persuaded Courtenay to go to the West. (After the close of Chapter 6 are two maps that should give some idea as to Wyatt's movements and area's where proclamations were made.)

On Thursday, 25 January, Wyatt published a proclamation at Maidstone against the Queen's marriage and desired that all his neighbors, friends, and all Englishmen join with him and others to defend their realm from the danger of strangers invading and ruling their kingdom. Thomas Wyatt met with George Harper, who had already given his word of support, in Rochester, where they made their proclamation and seized the bridge. They fortified the east part of the town with no opposition. Wyatt stationed men on the bridge who threatened anyone that passed that they should remain silent and not mention what they had just seen while on their way to London, taking only their weapons from them before allowing them to pass. Meanwhile, Henry Isleie (?) and others were busy trying to secure supporters in West Kent while others did the same in East Kent, issuing the same proclamation that Wyatt had while he was in Milton and Ashford and other towns in the region, which had stirred many people.

John Twine, Mayor of Canterbury, had indicated that, regardless of the diligent attempts of the heretics to raise the people, not one person outwardly joined Wyatt or any other of the heretics. Certainly there must have been a certain amount of people that now questioned the validity of what the heretics were saying, as the conspirators worked on the fears that many already had. It would seem as though a few from these towns would have joined at this point, because various accounts indicated that their numbers were increasing. Christopher Roper, a gentleman of Milton, challenged those who posted the proclamation and they quickly took him as a prisoner to Wyatt, who would know what to do with him. Two other gentlemen who also spoke out against the rebels were taken from their houses, also to Rochester, where they were held as prisoners with Roper.

Wyatt had written to Sir Robert Southwell, the Sheriff of Kent, requesting his support in "respect of the preservation of the common-wealth now in danger to be overrun of strangers through the presented marriage if it should go forward," and also for the support of Henry Neville, Lord Abergavenny, who would be a great asset to the cause if he chose to join. When Henry Neville received Wyatt's request he quickly reported it to the Queen. The Queen responded to Neville's information and news that rebellions had began in Kent by writing to Elizabeth, preparing her to either come to the Queen of her own accord, or be brought to her; it was her choice. The letter, though congenial has certain undertones:

Right dear and entirely beloved sister,

We greet you well: and whereas certain evil-disposed persons, minding more the satisfaction of their own malicious and seditious minds than their duty of allegiance towards us, have of late solely spread divers lewd and untrue rumors; and by that means and other devilish practices do travail to induce our good and loving subjects to an unnatural rebellion against God, us and the tranquility of our realm: We tendering the surety of your person, which might chance to be in some peril if any sudden tumult should arise where you now be, or about Donnington, whither, as we understand, you are minded shortly to remove, do therefore think expedient you should put yourself in good readiness, with all convenient speed, to make your repair hither to us. Which we pray you fail not to do: Assuring you, that as you may most safely remain here, so shall you be most heartily welcome to us. And of your mind herein we pray you to return answer by this messenger.

Given under our signet at our manor of St. James's the 26th of January in the 1st year of our reign.

Your loving sister,

Mary the Queen. [Aikin, pg. 139]

The letter arrived to find Elizabeth sick and confined in bed, and her officers sent a formal reply indicating that fact to the Queen. They had also attempted to express their concern to the Princess that any delay in fulfilling her sister's request may be misconstrued. The French Ambassador de Noailles had said that Elizabeth's illness was "a favorable illness," as to avoid any punishment from her sister.

Robert Southwell and George Clerk assembled those who were remaining loyal to the Queen and departed for Malling on Saturday, 27 January. Upon their arrival, they read an exhortation that Southwell wrote for the occasion informing everyone not to listen to the traitor Wyatt. They declared that Wyatt and his followers were traitors and would be punished as such. Very shortly after the counter-proclamation was issued in Malling, Henry Isleie and others were at Tonbridge, where they proclaimed that the Sheriff, Lord Abergavenny, and George Clerk were traitors to God, the Crown, and all who where living in the realm for rising the Queens subjects, and to defend the evil enterprise of the wicked members of the Council. They then declared in their names and Wyatt's that they were true and faithful servants of the realm. They then departed Tonbridge for Sevenoaks to issue a proclamation, and from there they would march onto Rochester. On the same day, the Queen had dispatched a messenger who arrived in Rochester but could not proceed any further than the bridge. He informed the rebels that the Queen was offering a pardon to any man who would separate himself from the heretics, return within twenty-four hours to their homes, and remain quiet citizens.

Henry Neville, Lord Abergavenny, the Sheriff, Warren Sentleger, and others were assembled within four miles of Rochester, in Malling, on Saturday night. Having received information that Henry Isleie and five-hundred Welshmen were at Sevenoaks, Neville prepared for a confrontation. Apparently Isleie planned to march towards Rochester in the morning to assist Wyatt against the forces of the Duke of Norfolk, who was in route to Gravesend from London with members of the guard and five-hundred "white coats" (a term given to London trained bands wearing a kind of uniform taken from the English national flag with a red cross of Saint George).

Early in the morning of 28 January, the Lord Abergavenny, the sheriff and several other gentlemen leading a force of about five hundred armed men, departed Malling all marching in perfect military fashion.

Abergavenny and his forces stopped at Wrotham Heath and waited until they heard the sounds of the drums of their enemies, which they soon did in the near distance, and they quickly departed towards them in great haste.

The Lord Abergavenny had stationed his forces at a place called Barrow Green, which is described as being on the way from Sevenoaks towards George Clerks house. Lord Abergavenny positioned his men in strategic locations and prepared either to overtake or to give pursuit if required. Somehow, Isleie's forces knew of Abergavenny's location and slipped around their position before the Lord Abergavenny had a chance to react. When Abergavenny's forces did finally respond, his foot soldiers were unable to keep up with the pace. Isleie's forces had ascended Wrotham Hill and, feeling that they had the advantage by winning the hill, displayed their ensigns, believing that they were out of danger. However, Abergavenny's men had pursued them with such haste that they encountered them about a mile from the hill at Blacksoll field.

Both sides exchanged shot and arrows wounding several, but no accounts of death were recorded. Abergavenny's horsemen charged Isleie's forces, which scattered and were chased for four miles to Hartley Wood, were many were taken prisoner. Isleie's remaining forces fled to save their lives. Though there are no real indications of the size of Abergavenny's forces, it must have been close to the size of Isleie's, or possibly greater, as they were quick to overtake them. Isleie fled to Hampshire, and his accomplices had fled so quickly that they arrived in Rochester that evening. At about the same point in time, George Harper, who heard of the Duke of Norfolk's advancing forces, had fled from Wyatt's location to surrender himself to the duke that had arrived at Gravesend and accepted Harper's surrender.

On the morning of Monday, 29 January, the Duke of Norfolk's forces, which consisted mostly of 200 Londoners, and members of the guard, marched toward Strood in a cold rain, where they arrived at about four o'clock. Several gentlemen of rank were with them, including the captain of the guard and the Bishop of Rochester, esquires and knights. Five captains remained behind, indicating that they would protect the Duke's rear from any enemy attack while the Duke set up his ordinance further ahead.

When Norfolk charged his ordinance and went into Rochester, he found Wyatt displaying his ensigns with no regard to his appearance. Norfolk commanded a shot be fired into Rochester, and as the gunner fired, a man ran to the Duke and told him how the Londoners would betray him. The five captains and their forces that had remained behind did just that, and as Norfolk turned around he was met with loud shouts of, "We are all Englishmen, we are all Englishmen." They quickly positioned themselves in a defensive posture in the shape of an arch and pointed their weapons at the Duke. Norfolk, sensing the danger, ordered his entire ordinance that was pointed towards Rochester be turned towards his new enemy. Perhaps realizing he was outnumbered, Norfolk did not fire a shot, and with the captain of the guard at his side, he realized that they now had enemies behind them and now in front of them, and moved his remaining forces aside.

Thomas Wyatt, accompanied by two or three men, had come forward about a half a mile from Rochester to meet the five captains and George Harper. As they approached each other, each gave the other a hand salute, and both forces joined into one. Then they marched into Rochester. By now, the Sheriff had fled to Maidstone, but received word to meet the Lord Abergavenny at Malling as quickly as he could. Upon his arrival, Abergavenny quickly departed for London to seek advice and guidance from the Council.

On the same day, a mailbag from the French Ambassador to the king was seized. Among the letters was a copy of the letter sent by Elizabeth to the Queen on 26 January further arousing suspicions that she was maintaining contact with the French King. Renard again insisted that the Queen should strongly consider bringing Elizabeth to London and confine her in the Tower. Meanwhile the Duke of Suffolk had not made contact with his family for quite some time, and the Duchess had sent numerous messengers but was unable to locate him. Lady Jane and her mother began to fear that he had become involved in the numerous protests that were occurring.

Henry Grey, the Duke of Suffolk, had so far been reluctant to make his proclamations in the Northern areas, but when the news arrived that Wyatt had secured a major victory, his brothers and he rode with great haste to the town of Leicester and made the same proclamation that Wyatt had. However, he did not receive the support he had hoped for because no one was willing to join him, or for that matter listen to him. It was reported that Thomas Dannett of Brodegate assembled an esti- mated 400 men at Leicester, armed and ready to serve the cause, but Suffolk soon found that this was not true. Suffolk and about five others rode to Coventry, a town they were told that would support them when they arrived. However, they were unaware that the Queen had sent the Earl of Huntington, who had already spoken to the town and prepared them with armor and arms to keep Suffolk from entering the city. It was here that they learned why the people of Leicester were not open to their presence.

Discouraged and apprehensive to proceed, and finding no support in the two shires of Leicester and Warwick, they departed to the Duke's manor in Astley, which was about five miles from Coventry, where they determined that the best action to take was for each man to go his own way. The remaining money was distributed between them with the amount depending on their rank, and Suffolk and his brother rode to a place called Astley Park. The Earl of Huntington had picked up their trail and pursued them into Coventry. He eventually found the Duke of Suffolk hiding in a hollowed out tree and his brother John inside a bail of hay. Huntington took his prisoners, seized all their money and possessions, and headed for London. Suffolk's brother Thomas is said to have fled to France, but was captured when he returned to claim his money and his cap that he had forgotten in a room in the inn at which he spent the night. Thomas was also taken as a prisoner to London, where he would later account for his actions.

Mary was still unable to get the Council to provide her with men-at-arms, or even a guard to offer her protection as news of Wyatt's advancement caused her some concern, as the she was unsure of just who she could trust. Renard did his best to see that the Queen was well guarded. Wyatt, now confident with his victory, removed six pieces of ordinance from the Queen's ships that where anchored in the Thames River. Renard informed the Emperor that a source close to him had information that a Venetian ship had come into the harbor and that the captain had given Wyatt five or six pieces of artillery at the encouragement of the Venetian Ambassador. His source was not completely sure of this information and could not affirm it. Nevertheless, Wyatt assembled his pieces of ordinance and with his large force left Rochester towards London. They arrived at Cowling Castle, about four miles outside Rochester, knowing that the Lord Cobham was there. Wyatt fired his cannons at the gate, eventually destroying it.

The Lord Cobham tried to defend the castle the best that he could with only a few others who remained behind. Cobham had wounded a couple of Wyatt's men with pistol shots, and two of his own men were killed before he surrendered to Wyatt, realizing that he could not go up against so many. It is not clear what Wyatt did with Cobham, other than they had a long discussion. Then Wyatt departed for Gravesend then marched on, spending the night at Dartford. While there, Edward Hastings and Thomas Cornwallis, who were both acting as representatives of the Queen's Privy Council, visited them. They requested that Wyatt tell them what he had hoped to do. After Wyatt's response, Hastings then accused Wyatt of being a traitor and not a true subject as he was telling people in his proclamations.

Wyatt stepped forward and said that he was not a traitor but was only defending the kingdom from unwelcome strangers. He then made several demands to both members of the Council; he wanted custody of the Tower with the Queen inside it as a prisoner, and he would replace several counselors and place his own men in their positions. After a long conference, Hastings told Wyatt, "Before thou shall have thy traitorous demand granted, thou shall die and twenty thousand with thee." On this the counselors returned to London with Wyatt's response, where the Queen immediately responded by issuing a proclamation informing everyone that Suffolk's men had been scattered and Peter Carew had fled to France.

On that same day of 1 February, news arrived in London about Wyatt's approach to the city, and the foreign Ambassadors quickly fled by the Thames River in the opposite direction from the impending danger. In the afternoon, the Council informed the Queen that she should reinforce the Tower, leave Westminster, and go to Guildhall. The Queen was escorted by members of the Council, the guard, and several gentlemen, including Courtenay, to Guildhall, where she gave a speech to the people declaring that Wyatt was a traitor who would tyrannize and molest the people and that he had taken up arms against the crown. She declared that her decision to marry a foreigner was a decision that was made by the Council for the best welfare of the kingdom, not of her own personal desires. Mary continued in her speech that she requested all to behave like good subjects, and if they did, she would stand with them to the very end, for this time their very fortunes, safety, wives, and children were in danger if Wyatt was allowed to continue. She urged them to take up arms against him and prevent him from entering the city.

Mary's speech had apparently motivated the crowd because they cried out loudly that they would support her and they declared Wyatt a traitor. When Mary's speech was read in other nearby towns, the reactions were the same, and many armed themselves with what they could and prepared for Wyatt's arrival. It was mentioned in a letter that Renard had written to the Emperor that five hundred of Wyatt's followers changed sides after the Queen's speech. The Queen also issued a proclamation promising that a reward of one hundred crowns would be paid to anyone who either arrested or killed Wyatt and brought him to London. Immediately after the speech, the Queen sent a messenger to inform Pembroke to change his direction and to seek out and capture Wyatt.

On the same day, Wyatt, now with fourteen ensigns and with an estimate of four thousand men, marched to Detford Strand and was within four miles of London when news arrived of the Queen's speech. The people's reaction caused Wyatt to stop his forces and stay the night and the entire following day. His advisers told him that they had stopped longer than they felt comfortable and could not afford to wait any longer. This was perhaps Wyatt's one real tactical error, because his delay allowed the Queen time to reinforce her cause and forces.

Thomas Gresham, while in Antwerp, wrote a letter to the Council reporting that Sir John Mason visited on 2 February, and advised not to send any money along the seas because of reports about the rebels and the presence of some French ships of war off the coast. A payment that was to be transported was also held because of news that Wyatt's forces were ready with a large force of foot soldiers to attack London. Also about this time, a servant of the Duke of Suffolk had been caught carrying a placard issued by the Duke that was to be distributed in various locations declaring that there were twelve thousand Spaniards at Calais and more in the West Country ready to invade England and that the people should take up arms against them. The man was later hanged for his crimes.

On Saturday, 3 February, Wyatt marched to Southwark, where he found the gate closed on the London Bridge, and he dispatched some of his men to look for another path in Winchester. That night the London Bridge was guarded by three hundred men led by the Lord William Howard, Lord Admiral of England, and Lord Mayor Sir Thomas White, who ordered that the drawbridge be removed and thrown into the Thames River to prevent Wyatt from entering London. Wyatt had considered removing a wall from a nearby house near the bridge to connect the gap between themselves and London. They chose to wait several hours and return later to see if the other side was not such a flurry of activity. They did return at about eleven o'clock to find the sentry in a slumber, and they then proceeded to bridge the gap. Wyatt woke the sentry and told him to remain still or lose his life; he was happy to remain quiet.

As Wyatt reached the other side, he found the Lord Admiral, the Lord Mayor, Sir Andrew Judd, and a couple of others discussing how they successfully secured the bridge. Wyatt listened for a moment before returning to his men and told them that the place was too hot and that it would not be safe to cross. They discussed other plans, including returning to Greenwich, where they could cross over and meet other supporters from London. Several other options were reviewed, and it was clear that they could not turn around because the Lord Abergavenny and his forces where coming from Rochester.

On Sunday, 4 February, Wyatt observed that the bridge was fortified by shifts of three hundred guards stationed there night and day. Wyatt was more concerned at how they were resisting him rather than the number of them, and left Southwark before six in the morning and marched towards Kingston, arriving there at about four o'clock in the afternoon to find about thirty feet of the bridged removed. He then decided that two should attempt to swim over to a barge and return with it; then others could cross over on it, which they did while others were stealing planks and beams from anywhere they could find them and build their own crossing. They completed building and moving all his men and ordinance at about eleven o'clock that night, and headed straight for London. The Earl of Pembroke, General of the Queen's army, discovered them just before day-break with a large and impressive force in St. James field beside Westminster. The Earl's men immediately moved into a defensive posture and prepared all their artillery and archers for battle, who would be under the charge of the Lord Clinton, now Marshal of the field. The two forces collided and the battle began as artillery came to life. Wyatt changed direction and tired to move towards St. James, only to find that the Queen's horsemen were pursuing him on two sides. They quickly charged into Wyatt's ranks, scattering some of them in different directions. Wyatt then tried several different ways to enter London, but each was as heavily fortified as the next, and with less than one hundred men remaining, he stopped at the gate of the Temple Barr, amazed at how well defended London was, and agreed to surrender to Sir Maurice Barkie, a knight who just happen to be riding by.

After surviving several battles and skirmishes in which some were killed and many wounded, and after many miles of marching in the cold, rain, and sleet, Wyatt finally entered the heavily fortified and guarded city of London, as a prisoner.

Chapter 4. February 1554 – April 1555. Bloody Mary

There are several things to be said about Thomas Wyatt the younger. He had learned a great deal while serving as a captain with King Henry VIII in France, as his father did, and both were noted as worthy soldiers. In this, his final campaign, he overcame many obstacles, including the weather, and accomplished a great deal in a short period. Wyatt was so strong in his convictions and sure of the threat that he posed that he caused the Queen to move from Westminster to Guildhall as a precaution and he had advanced to within a mile and a half of the Queen. Had it not been for the lack of support, the outcome could have been much different. Wyatt could not have seen into the future, but the Spanish did in fact invade England, thirty-four years later in the Spanish Armada. Mary, with a certain amount of luck, sound advice, and her calm nature under pressure, proved that she was a formidable leader who managed to stay just one step ahead of Wyatt, thus preventing a major coup from occurring.

Rejoicing that the rebellion had finally ended, the Ambassadors left after speaking of the Queen's lack of money to Simon

Renard, who in turn informed the Emperor in his letter of 5 February. Renard had also requested, on the Queen's behalf, a sum of two hundred thousand crowns that the Queen would repay with interest. Previously, Mary had indicated to Renard that her fleet was not large enough or equipped to defeat the French by themselves, and if they wanted to be able to prevent a war, she requested that the Emperor combine fleets with hers.

Mary had other concerns also. She had to sort through hundreds of prisoners and ensure that they received a fair trial, as well as prevent any further problems. In the presence of the Queen only, Renard questioned the Chancellor, attempting to gain his opinion as to what should be done about Courtenay's name being mentioned in the intercepted French Ambassadors letters, but the Chancellor did not reply. When Renard had showed the Chancellor his decipherment of the letters, Renard informed the Emperor that the Chancellor changed color so obviously, that it was clear what was on his mind. Courtenay's involvement with Wyatt had already been questioned, but a couple of days after his capture, Thomas Wyatt confessed during questioning that both Courtenay and Princess Elizabeth were involved in the rebellion. A theory exists that Wyatt may have done this in a vain attempt to have his life spared if he were to reveal important information to the Queen, such as Courtenay and Elizabeth's involvement.

As things began to settle around the Queen, Mary began the preparations for Philip's arrival, which was planned for July. Mary had sent a letter to the Emperor requesting the number of people that were to accompany Philip to England. The Emperor responded that he was unable to give precise numbers but he estimated that there would be about three thousand total for the household and Court and about six thousand for all who were serving with the fleet, including the sailors, but only about three thousand would actually come on land, with about fifteen hundred horses and mules.

In a letter of 8 February, Renard again brought to the Emperor's attention that Mary's lack of money was causing her a great deal of concern and she was unable to collect on the four thousand to five thousand crowns owed to her and feared that she would not be able to defend herself in the event of an attack. The Queen tried to keep her financial situation a secret because if that information leaked out, any of her enemies would surely take advantage of the situation. Several circumstances led to her present financial problems, including past and present military campaigns and the Queen's inability to collect on the debts owed to her, resulting in a state of desperation that is very clear in various correspondences. This depletion of funds appeared to be a result of recent events because it had been recorded that Mary did pay all debts related to the death of her brother, Edward VI.

Renard informed the Emperor that most of the heretics were now in prison, but there had been no decision regarding Courtenay and Elizabeth. Courtenay's departure was suspended as a result of the recent problems, and because the treaty of alliance had been ratified, there was no longer a reason to send Courtenay away, but the Emperor indicated to Renard that he would consider it in the future if the opportunity arose.

Renard, summoned by the Queen early in the morning of 12 February, was informed that the Council had issued orders for Courtenay's immediate arrest and that he was to be taken to the Tower under guard as a prisoner. The Council's decision was based on Wyatt's "unmolested" accusations that Courtenay, Elizabeth and others, such as Pickering and Carew, who had escaped capture by fleeing to France, were involved in the past conspiracy. Having no response from Elizabeth, and now coupled with the serious insinuations made by Wyatt of

Courtenay and Elizabeth's involvement in the rebellion, Renard and the Council recommended that Mary should seize the opportunity to imprison both Courtenay and Elizabeth to prevent any further problems from arising. Mary acted swiftly to apprehend the Princess, and ordered the Council to send two of her personal physicians to determine whether Elizabeth was truly sick or just pretending to be. If she was not sick, Hastings and Cornwallis were to arrest her, take her to London, and place her in the Tower as a prisoner.

Tensions continued to remain high in the kingdom regardless of the suppression of the rebellion and imprisonment of the heretics. Many foreigners in the kingdom were now regarded as outcasts and chose to flee England after the doors on their houses were marked, instead of remaining to defend against attacks on themselves or family members or the ransacking and pilferage of their homes. As the capture of the remaining heretics continued, a reliable source indicated that Peter Carew was in fact in France, and the Queen responded quickly by sending a summons to France demanding his extradition immediately. Having the last major figure of the recent rebellion in prison would give closure to the event.

With Wyatt and his accomplices now in the Tower, Mary began the rather arduous task of executing those who were prosecuted for their involvement in the uprising and all those who opposed and stood against her. It is through her actions that she would earn the nickname "Bloody Mary," a description that would forever describe her handling of the heretics during a very turbulent period in English history. Mary had to do what was necessary to retain the upper hand. Of the many who were executed, the two most noteworthy were Lady Jane and her husband, who were executed late in the morning of Monday, 12 February 1554, on the Tower Green. Mary's decision to execute the sixteen-year-old Lady Jane and her husband was secured by her father's involvement in Wyatt's rebellion. Had it not been for his involvement, Lady Jane and her husband may have only been required to serve a small amount of time in prison before returning to a private life.

This Monday was called "Black Monday," and an unknown gentleman recorded the events that took place on that day in notes that were later published in the *Historical Memorials, Ecclesiastical and Civil, of events under the reign of Queen Mary I*, by John Strype in a 1721 edition.

> Thus this Black Monday began, with the Execution of this most Noble and Virtuous Lady and her Husband. On the same day, for a terrifying Sight, were many new Pairs of Gallows set up in London. As at every Gate one, two pair in Cheapside, one in Fleet Street, one in Smithfield, one in Holborn, one at Leadenhall, one at St. Magnus, one at Billingsgate, one at Pepper Alley Gate, one at St. George's, one in Barnsby Street, one on Tower Hill, one at Charing Cross, and one at Hide Park Corner. These gallows remained standing until Wednesday when men were hanged on every Gibbet, and some quartered also. In Cheapside six; at Aldgate one, hanged and quartered; at Leadenhall three; at Bishopgate one, and was quartered; at Moorgate one, and he was quartered; at Ludgate one and he was quartered; at Billingsgate three hanged; at St. Magnus three hanged; at Tower Hill three hanged; at Holborn three hanged; at Fleet Street three hanged; at Paul's Churchyard four; at Pepper Alley Corner three; at Barneby Street three; at St. George's three; at Charing Cross four; whereof two belonged to the Court; at Hidepark Corner three, one of them named Pollard, a water bearer. Those three were hanged in chains. But seven were quartered, and their bodies and heads set upon the gates of London.

That evening Courtenay was found and arrested in the Earl of Sussex's house by the Lord Chamberlain, who was accompanied by members of the guard. It was also discovered that Courtenay had in his possession several disguises, and it was assumed that he might have used them to escape capture by fleeing with Peter Carew. The anxiety of returning to the Tower must have been tremendous.

During the third week of February and beginning at the time of the execution of Lady Jane, an estimate of two hundred rebels were condemned. One hundred of them were executed locally and the remainder were sent to Kent, where they were hanged in the villages they rose in revolt. In London, executions took place in about twenty to thirty different locations. On the 13th, thirty soldiers and small number of gentlemen were executed, and the following day, thirteen more were executed. Shortly after Courtenay was placed in the Tower, the Queen banned his mother, the Marchioness of Exeter, who was once close to the Queen, from all the activities of Court. The Council was not taking any chances by allowing the mother of a man suspected of committing treasonous acts so close to the Queen.

Renard described to the Emperor that wherever one went in London, they saw gibbets and the bodies of the hanged. The stench of the rotting corpses was overwhelming as their bodies where displayed throughout London and several heads were displayed above the city gates. It was also about this time that forty soldiers that had abandoned the Duke of Norfolk were hanged, and two hundred additional had been sentenced to receive the same. It was decided that Wyatt's execution could not take place until he had been confronted by Princess Elizabeth, who was still too sick to travel more than about six miles a day. It was suggested that she was pregnant, and a few suspected that it was possibly Courtenay's child.

At the Emperor's request, Renard investigated Mary's money problems. In a letter to the Emperor dated 13 February, Renard mentions the poor state of Mary's financial condition and that there was no one who maintained the budget, leaving her without money or credit. Renard reminded the Queen of the previous advice given by the Emperor that she had paid all the debts of the late King Edward VI and should seek credit in Antwerp.

Between 13 and 15 February, Courtenay was questioned without the presence of his mother, which may have influenced matters differently, and he continued to deny his involvement in the rebellion and charges that were brought against him, only confessing that a servant of his had fled to France of his own will and against his (Courtenay's) own. During that period of time, Courtenay received a letter from Angelo Mariano of Italy congratulating him on his newly acquired freedom and the restoration of his honors, and that he would recommend him for employment and that any provision allowed by the Crown may be paid to his agent. Ironically, this letter would have arrived to find Courtenay again a prisoner in the Tower.

News arrived at Court on 17 February that Peter Carew had visited the French Court and that the King was asked to declare him a traitor and ban him from France or it may appear that he was hiding and abetting a rebel. The French King responded that he did not know a Peter Carew, nor did he visit him at Court, and that the French King wished to remain friends and at peace with the Queen. Renard does not disclose his source, but he indicated that Carew was motivated by religion and Courtenay had promised to follow the new religion when married to Elizabeth and placed on the throne. Shortly after, news arrived at Court from the Deputy of Calais, who indicated that Carew received three ships and was made a Colonel by the French King and given command of one thousand English troops in France to fight against the Queen. The king had also contributed about twelve thousand crowns to several private persons and had promised help in additional money and troops. On the same day, Renard informed the Emperor that he had received information from the King of France that Cardinal Alessandro, Farnese, grandson of Pope Paul III, said he had seen Courtenay, or someone with a strong resemblance to him, in Paris several weeks before his arrest and confinement on 12 February.

In an attempt to prevent the possibility of those with like ideas from rising in the future, a public proclamation was issued similar to the one the Queen issued on 19 July ordering all of the foreigners who took refuge in England after committing crimes of some sort in their homeland to leave England or be subjected to punishment. Meanwhile, the Duke of Suffolk was detained and condemned for committing treason by joining and promoting the efforts of Thomas Wyatt. He was beheaded six days later on the very spot that his daughter had lost her head.

The following day, the Emperor wrote several letters of appreciation addressed to the Earl of Pembroke, Earl of Derby, Earl of Shrewsbury, Bishop of Winchester, Sir Robert Rochester, Sir William Petre, the Bishop of Durham, the Earl of Arundel, and Lord Paget for the valiant and faithful services they rendered to the Queen and his son Philip in suppressing the rebellion. The Emperor also announced that he was sending the Prince of Gavre, Count d'Egmont, to thank them on his behalf. Twenty-two more copies of the letter were written but not addressed, with four beginning, "My cousin"; twelve beginning, "Very dear and good friend"; and the remaining six with, "Reverend father in God, our very dear and good friend."

On the same day, the Emperor wrote a letter to Mary informing her that he was sending the Count d'Egmont with news and instructions that he recommended she follow. The Emperor also informed Count d'Egmont that he was to leave for England, and informed him that intercepted letters of the French Ambassador had shown that the conspirators were either working with or for Courtenay and Elizabeth and at the very least the Queen should consider confining both of them in the Tower, not knowing that Courtenay had already been. As for Courtenay, the Emperor recommended that if the Council did not have enough evidence to convict him that a second plan should be put in place by sending him to Spain for some reason that would not arise suspicion on his part. The Emperor concluded by stating that England would be better off without Courtenay.

Most of the Council and the Queen agreed that if Courtenay could not be convicted that he should be sent out of the kingdom. Those that had any doubts changed their minds as news of the French plots arrived that indicated that Courtenay and Elizabeth would seize the Queen, place her in the Tower, and then execute her and claim the throne. These plots were said to be orchestrated by Peter Carew, Wyatt, Crofts, and Thomas Grey, brother of the late Duke of Suffolk. It was also revealed that the King of France had already distributed a great deal of money to private individuals in support of the rebellion.

Partly to appease the concerns that many still had regarding a foreigner (Philip) reigning in their kingdom, it was decided that a session of Parliament should be held to approve and ratify the marriage treaty between Mary and Philip as soon as possible. The necessary letters were drawn and sent to the various provinces, as it was customary to announce a session of Parliament six weeks before they would meet. The Queen had hoped to try, convict, and serve punishment on as many of the heretics as possible before Parliament was to meet and 40 more men were hanged and many more condemned to the same punishment. The numbers of prisoners increased as more were located and captured. Renard sent the Emperor a list of the prisoners in the Tower that were held for crimes they committed during the last conspiracy in a letter of 24 February. Among the forty-five names were the Duke of Suffolk, the Marquess of Northampton, the Earl of Devon, Lord John Grey, Lord Thomas Grey, Lord Cobham, Thomas Wyatt, Gawen Carew, and Peter Carew, who was at the time a refugee. This list contained mostly knights, some gentlemen, and a priest. About half were already sentenced and a few executed, like the Duke of Suffolk.

Courtenay had continued to reaffirm his innocence and said that he had no involvement with the conspirators, so the Council decided within the first couple of days of March that Courtenay would be allowed to confront Wyatt with the presence of three witnesses. Courtenay was brought to Wyatt's chamber and in the presence of the witnesses and members of the guard, Wyatt maintained his original accusations that he had devised, assembled, and led the rebellion on Courtenay's behalf and that Courtenay was as much of a traitor as he was. Courtenay vehemently denied all that Wyatt had said and was then escorted back to his chamber in the Tower.

As the prisoners in the Tower were questioned, some would implement others, as we have already seen. Renard wrote to the Emperor with important news gathered upon the capture of Crofts, who confessed that the French Ambassador had an understanding with the heretics and rebels, and Renard promised to send a copy of the confession that could very well be used to prove the dishonesty of the French. A gentleman who was believed to have fled to France with Peter Carew was captured, and later that day while in confinement he tried to commit suicide by thrusting a butter knife into his stomach, but he was unsuccessful and afterwards confessed to assisting in the plot to kill the Queen.

Within the next few days, several prisoners in the Tower had come forward with accusations of Courtenay's involvement in the plot: that he had a cipher that was carved on a guitar that was to be used with Peter Carew, that the whole plot was done on his behalf, and that he had been in communication with the King of France, all of which were serious charges. Nevertheless, the English Parliament had already laid down the law that the capital punishment could not be awarded to those who had only consented to the act of treason if they had committed no overt act, but could only be sentenced to life imprisonment. Without evidence that Courtenay had in fact violated that statute, he could not be executed, something for which many wished.

Setting aside the unsubstantiated claims that many historians have made regarding Courtenay's involvement in Wyatt's rebellion, one early historian indicates a point in which I agree on. After having spent slightly half of his life imprisoned in the Tower, it would be safe to speculate that Courtenay would have enjoyed his new freedom, and it seems very unlikely that he would have done anything to jeopardize it, especially by committing the most severe of acts, as treason (by joining or leading those in a rebellion against the Queen) would be. Further evidence to support Courtenay's lack of involvement could be the thorough investigation that would have resulted from Thomas Wyatt's accusation upon his capture of Courtenay and Elizabeth's involvement. History has recorded no ill results of any findings, and the fact that Courtenay was eventually released from the Tower with his head could in part lend some credence to his innocence.

Princess Elizabeth was questioned also by the Chancellor, Arundel, Petre, and Paget, and among the questions, they inquired about the son of the Lord Privy Seal, who had confessed to delivering letters to Elizabeth from Wyatt during the rebellion. The Princess denied knowledge of these activities and after this line of questioning; the Privy Seal was very upset that his only son was implicated with Elizabeth.

The mood of London as a result of the recent rebellion and now of the numerous executions left the city in a state of pandemonium, this can be viewed by a rather interesting event that occurred about 9 March in which an estimate of three hundred children of various ages had gathered in a field somewhere in or around London, then divided themselves into two groups; one representing the Queen, and the other representing Wyatt. Then they acted out the quarrel in a way they believed had occurred between the Queen and Wyatt, with several children on both sides hurt and even wounded. Many were arrested and placed in Guildhall. On the same day, Thomas Grey, the younger brother of the Duke of Suffolk, was condemned to death.

On 11 March, a servant of Courtenay was caught visiting John Younge, who was regarded as one of the leaders of the rebellion and a servant of the French Ambassador. It has been suggested that the servant attempted to persuade Younge to keep the secret and not to accuse Courtenay of his involvement. This led to Walgrave cross-examining the servant at the request of the Chancellor, and the following day Courtenay's servant was given his liberty despite the jailer's objections, who had heard his confession. Renard complained to the Emperor in a letter of 14 March that the trials of Courtenay and Elizabeth were being poorly handled, which made him suspicious because of the delays that appeared to him as being on purpose hoping that something would arise that may save them. Renard points out to the Emperor that the Queen had no say in the matter because it was being managed by the Chancellor, who had even appointed a gentleman to guard and question the prisoners in the Tower that supported the Queen's marriage to Courtenay. Renard described this gentleman as being one of the most ignorant, corrupt, and violent Englishman alive. By now, Courtenay had also been moved from his first place of imprisonment to another more comfortable one by the Chancellor without an order by the Council to do so.

With the threats of certain heretics now passed, the Queen considered letting go all of the troops in her forces except for about five hundred that were currently under the command of Lord Henry Strange. Mary did this mainly in an attempt to save precious money, as her recent expenditures exceeded her income. Talk of holding Parliament in Oxford had many Londoners upset at the thought of losing income if they were to meet elsewhere. Now coupled with the additional concerns, the Council persuaded the Queen not to leave London until the trials of Courtenay and Elizabeth were completed and Parliament had concluded its session.

Early in the morning of 14 March, some of the heretics, still dissatisfied even after the fall of Wyatt, had a man and a woman stir the people in London by claiming that a voice of an angel could be heard from within a wall of their house. When those who had gathered to witness the event said, "God save Queen Mary," there was no response from the voice. When they said "God save the Lady Elizabeth," the voice replied, "So be it." Then the question of, "what is Mass?" was asked and the voice responded "idolatry." By about eleven in the morning, an estimate of seventeen thousand people had gathered around the house and caused quite a commotion. The Council quickly dispatched the Admiral, Paget, and the Captain of the Guard to arrest the couple. Though their exact motivations were never recorded, it was believed the couple did so by request to stir sympathy towards the prisoners Elizabeth and Courtenay and to excite the people against the Queen.

By ten o'clock in the evening, the Queen's doctors had arrived at Ashridge with three members of the Council: Sir Richard Southwell, Sir Edward Hastings, and Sir Thomas Cornwallis. They arrived to find the Princess in bed, and she refused to receive them but they entered her bedchamber anyway and declared they were there by order from the Queen. A visibly upset Elizabeth complained about this harsh treatment as the doctors began their examination of the Princess. Dr. Owen and Dr. Wendy decided that the Princess could travel without the possibility of endangering herself, and dressed comfortably, she departed her childhood home of Ashridge that her father had purchased as a nursery for her and her brother Edward, in a litter provided by the Queen. They traveled about five miles on the first day, arriving in Redborn, a town about seven miles south of Luton. That evening Elizabeth was still weak and very displeased about being forced to take the trip. On the second day, they traveled about five more miles, possibly along Watling Street, arriving in St. Albans, where they received accommodations from Sir Ralph Rowlet for the night. The following day they traveled most likely along the same road for about five miles to the town of Mimms, where a Mr. Dod had agreed to accommodate them for the night. On the forth day, the weary and still upset Elizabeth arrived after another short journey of about five to six miles to Highgate, a village situated on high ground near Hampstead, were they spent the night and the following day, most likely so Elizabeth could regain her strength before completing the final leg of their journey into London.

Gardiner Bishop of Winchester was accompanied by nineteen members of the Council and addressed the still upset and sick Elizabeth with the charges of her not only being involved in Wyatt's conspiracy, but also of having part in the rebellion of Peter Carew. Elizabeth vehemently denied all accusations, but it was no use, and they dismissed her personal attendants and put the Queen's in their place. They informed her that it was by the desire of the Queen that she should be placed in the Tower. The following day, two Lords of the Council came to take the Princess to the Tower on a barge that was waiting. The Princess requested that they wait until the next day, but they would not agree to this and she then requested to be allowed to write to the Queen. At first, they would not permit that either, but after debating the issue, the Earl of Sussex permitted her to write the letter and said he would deliver it to the Queen and return an answer if one was given.

Of the many letters that Elizabeth wrote to the Queen during this period, I believe that the following reflects the strong emotions that the Princess was feeling as a result of the anxieties from a long, tedious trip from her childhood home and now with the news that she would be placed in the Tower on charges that could most likely mean her death.

To the Queen.

If any ever did try this olde saynge, that a Kinge's worde was more than another man's othe, I most humbly beseeche your majesty to verefie it in me, and to remember your last promis and my last demande, that I be not condemned without answer and due porfe: wiche it semes that now I am, for that without cause provid I am by your counsel frome you commanded to go unto the Tower; a place more wonted for a false traitor, than a tru subject. Wiche thogth I knowe I deserve it not, yet in the face of al this realme aperes that it is provid; wiche I pray God, I may dy the shamefullist dethe that ever any died, afore I may mene any suche thinge: and to this present hower I protest afor God (who shal juge my trueth, whatsoever malice shal devis) that I never practiced, consiled, not consented to any thinge that might be prejudicial to your parson an way, of daungerous to the state by any mene. And therfor I humbly beseche your mauestie to let me answer afore your selfe, and not suffer me to trust to your counselors; yea and that afore I go to the Tower, if it be possible; if not, afore I be further condemned. Howbeit, I trust assuredly, your highness wyl give me leve to do it afor I go; for that thus I may not be cried out on, as now I shalbe; yea and without cause. Let consciens move your hithness to take some bettar way with me, than to make me be condemned in al mens sigth, afor my desert knowen. Also I most humbly deseche your higtthnes to pardon this my boldness, wiche innocency procures me to do, together with hope of your natural kindness; wiche I trust wyl not se me cast away without desert: wiche what it is, I wold desire no more of God, byt that you truly knewe. Wiche thinge I thinke and beleve you shal never by report knowe, unless by your selfe you hire. I have harde in my time of many cast away, for want of comminge to the presence of ther Prince: and in late days I harde my Lorde of Sommerset say, that if never sufferd: but the perwwaisions wer made to him so gret, that he was brogth in belefe that he coulde not live safely if the Admiral lived; and that made him give his consent to his dethe. Thougth thes parsons ar not to be comared to your majestie, yet I pray God, as ivel perswations perseade not one sistar again the other; and al for that the have harde false report, and not harkene to the trueth knowin. Therfor ons again, kniling with humbleness of my hart, because I am not sufferd to bow the knees of my body, I humbly crave to speke with your higthnis: wiche I wolde not be so bold to desire, if I knewe not my selfe most clere, as I knowe my selfe most tru. And as for the traitor Wiat, he might paraventur writ me a lettor: but, on my faithe, I never receved any from him. And as for the copie of my lettar sent to the Frenche Kinge, I pray God confound me eternally, it ever I sent him word, message, token, or lettar by any menes: and to this my truith I will stande in to my dethe.

Your highness most faithful subject that hathe bine from the beginne, and wylbe to my ende, Elizabeth. [Ellis, pg. 255-257]

Palm Sunday was a rainy, gloomy day, and as most people were at church, the barge transporting the Princess made its trip down the Thames River and arrived at the Traitors Gate, where Elizabeth refused to step onto the wharf. After several persuasions, she finally stepped onto the wharf saying, "Here landeth as true a subject, being prisoner, as ever landed at these stairs: and before thee O God I speak it, having none other friends but thee alone." The Princess was escorted to her prison chamber, were she fell into a deeper state of despair as the echoing of the door being closed, locked, and bolted reverberated in the halls of the dark and cold Tower. It was a long time before she was permitted to take any exercise outside her chamber.

Mary, her Council, and many others enjoyed a moment of relief because the rebellions had been suppressed, Wyatt, Courtenay, and Elizabeth were now in confinement, and plans for the arrival of Prince Philip could proceed. Raphael Holinshed has given a rather long and detailed account of Wyatt's trail, which took place about 8 or 9 April at Westminster before the Earl of Sussex, Sir Edward Hastings, Sir Thomas Cornwallis, and others who served as judges. Wyatt was charged with leading an armed force with ensigns displayed against the forces of the Queen with the intent to remove her from the throne by force if required. Thomas Wyatt responded that he was guilty and that he did what he had done because he was a free man and feared that the marriage between Mary and Philip was dangerous to the kingdom, as Philip would succeed the throne if Mary died and the kingdom would be brought into the bondage and servitude of aliens and strangers. Wyatt then asked that the Queen be merciful, and stated that no other subject in the kingdom was as truthful and faithful to her highness.

Wyatt gave examples of his faithful service to the Queen, such as serving the Queen against the Duke of Northumberland, and included his father's service with the King. He concluded that he had dishonored his family and understood that his actions may result in his death, but stood firm on his convictions, then again asked that her majesty be merciful. Edward Hastings then asked Wyatt why he had ignored the Queen's first offer of leniency, and he replied that he had already committed himself to the cause and had hoped at the very least to secure a treaty with the Queen. Hastings then asked him about a letter that he had written to the Duke of Suffolk requesting him to bring his forces and to meet him at Kingston Bridge. At first, Wyatt could not recall having written the letter, but when Hastings held the letter up, Wyatt confessed that he had done so. Wyatt continued to beg the Court and her majesty for leniency, but he realized that his would be an example to those with similar ideas in the future, and on that, the Court passed sentence that he would be hanged, drawn, and quartered, a penalty that was deserved of someone like himself.

On the day that Thomas Wyatt was to be executed, 11 April, he requested that the lieutenant of the Tower allow him to confront Courtenay, which he did in the presence of the lieutenant and Sheriffs. Wyatt fell to his knees in front of Courtenay and begged for his forgiveness because he had falsely accused both he and Elizabeth in his conspiracy. Wyatt was then taken from the Tower to the Tower Hill, and as he stood on the scaffold, Wyatt declared to the crowd that the Lady Elizabeth and Courtenay, both of which he had accused before, were never privy to his doings as far as he knew or was able to charge them. When Dr. Weston, being his confessor, told Wyatt that he had confessed the contrary to the Council Wyatt responded, "That I said then, but that which I say now is true." Wyatt was pardoned from the original sentence of drawing and hanging. Then his head was removed, his body quartered and placed in various locations in the city, and his head displayed upon the gallows beside Hide Park.

Immediately after Wyatt's execution, word was brought to the Lord Mayor that Wyatt had cleared the Lady Elizabeth and Courtenay and of the words he exchanged with Dr. Weston. As the Lord Mayor sat down to dinner, Martin Holmes and the Court recorder entered, having just come from the house of Parliament where reports of Wyatt's confession were read. Holmes informed everyone that there was an account that was contrary to what was told in the Parliament house. An apprentice and a servant of the Queen's had been overheard while drinking in a local pub discussing various topics, including Wyatt's confession of Elizabeth and Courtenay's innocence. Word of this conversation was reported to Bishop Gardiner, who dispatched a gentleman, commanding him to bring the apprentice to the Starchamber.

As the apprentice stood in the Starchamber listening to Gardiner declare how Mary had received her sister so tenderly and freed Courtenay and restoring his titles, for them to repay the Queen by conspiring treason against her with the traitor Wyatt that can be clearly seen by various letters. The Bishop then told the Lord Mayor that there were individuals in the city of London that stated that the Council had used various means to provoke Wyatt to accuse Elizabeth and Courtenay, but no one had been punished. The Lord Mayor responded, "The partie is here, take them with you," and then advised the Bishop that the city of London was a whirlpool of evil rumors and to take caution, for his action may have severe consequences.

At this point the lieutenant came forward, swearing that what he was about to say was the truth. He continued to describe when Wyatt confronted Courtenay in the Tower when he knelt down in front of him and begged that Courtenay should confess the truth and submit himself to the Queen's mercy.

There are no further accounts of this event in the Star-chamber, or of Wyatt's confession. Many members of the Council and other nobles believed Wyatt's original accusation of Elizabeth and Courtenay's involvement with Wyatt, but without conclusive evidence, the Princess and Edward would forever remain in the shadow of suspicion.

On 17 April, Nicholas Throckmorton was tried for treason and his involvement in Wyatt's rebellion. Numerous confessions had been read, including the Duke of Suffolk's, who had insinuated that Throckmorton was to join with Courtenay and meet Peter Carew to raise the counties of Devon and Cornwall. Throckmorton defended himself with great skill in a very colorful trial and was acquitted of all charges of treason. On 27 April, the Emperor received information that there was still no decision made regarding the punishment of Courtenay and Elizabeth, and the Emperor responded quickly by instructing Renard that there needed to be a decision made soon for the safety and well-being of the realm and kingdom. Regardless, the Emperor was pleased that the rebellion was over and most of those involved had been dealt with. As the Emperor was reassured that his son's safety was paramount, reports that a fleet of hoys (a small vessel often rigged as a sloop and used for short journeys) had been overtaken by French vessels. Seven where sunk, and the remainder had fled to the ports of Normandy.

Renard informed the Emperor in a letter of 1 May that the French Ambassador had complained to the Queen about two letters that he claimed were stolen from him in England. The Queen had only heard of one letter and turned to the Chancellor for an answer regarding the other. The Chancellor had indicated that he did in fact review the contents of the letter but he was unable to remember what he had done with it. He said that he had made an abstract of it and indicated that it mentioned that Courtenay was to marry Elizabeth and that the Queen was to lose the crown and her life. The letter mentioned that the pensioners would be against the Queen because they had not received their pensions for three years. Wyatt's plot had also been exposed.

The Queen revealed to Renard that it appeared that the Chancellor had purposely misplaced the letter to protect Courtenay and that he had also left Courtenay's name out of his translation of the other letter for the same reason. If the original letter could be located, it would be the one piece of evidence that would convict Courtenay and Elizabeth and condemn them to death. Nevertheless, the Queen summoned all the lawyers and chief Lords of the Council, who acted as judges and requested a report on the proceedings against Courtenay and their opinions on the matter. They had told the Queen that it was their opinion that Courtenay should be sentenced to death.

On the same day, Renard informed the Emperor that Courtenay was using a child of five years old, the son of one of the soldiers stationed in the Tower, to communicate with Elizabeth. The boy was immediately brought before several respected gentlemen for questioning and promised the reward of figs and apples. It has been suggested that the boy carried love letters and tokens from Courtenay to Elizabeth. The gentlemen asked the boy when he last visited the Earl of Devon. The boy answered that he would go "by and by thither." When asked when he last visited the Lady Elizabeth, the boy replied, "everyday." They then asked the boy what he carried from the Earl to Princess Elizabeth. The boy replied that he would go and find out what the Earl will give him to carry to her.

"This same is a crafty boy," said the Lord Chamberlain.

The boy then asked, "I pray you, my Lord, give me figs you promised me." The Lord Chamberlain quickly responded with "no, thou shall be whipped if thou come anymore to the Lady Elizabeth or the Lord Courtenay."

The boy answered, "I will bring my lady and mistress no more flowers." Upon this, the boy's father was commanded not to allow the boy to visit the chambers. The following day, as Princess Elizabeth walked in the garden, the boy cried to her through a hole in the door, "Mistress, I can bring no more flowers." Elizabeth smiled, understanding what they had done.

As preparations for Philip's arrival continued, tokens of appreciation were exchanged, and on 16 May, Prince Philip sent the Marquess de las Navas to visit the Queen in England and present her with a magnificent diamond as a present that the Emperor had given to his wife, Philip's mother.

Because of the incident with the boy in the Tower, discussion over what would be the best measure to prevent something like it from happening again resulted in a decision to separate Elizabeth and Courtenay. On Saturday, 19 May, Elizabeth was removed from the Tower and accompanied by four hundred men as they departed to Richmond and then on to Woodstock, about forty-five miles Northwest of London. As they passed along the street lined with people who rejoiced at what they believed to be Elizabeth being set free, several merchants shot off three cannons as a sign of joy. Those actions displeased the Council and the Queen, and several reprimands were issued as a result. It was decided that a different means would be required to move Courtenay, and on 25 May, Courtenay was removed from the Tower at three o'clock in the morning and escorted by Sir Thomas Treshan, the Chamberlain of Suffolk, and certain members of the Guard, then proceeded through London to Fotheringhay Castle, about eighty miles north of London, this time discreetly hoping to prevent a similar incident to Elizabeth's.

Also about this time, the split in the Council had made it to the public and accounts go as far as to say that they were hostile to one another and had forgotten their oath to the Queen in seeking vengeance. The Queen was informed that some individuals where in arms with the intent to take the Chancellor prisoner, but this did not proceed any further.

On 4 June, the Ambassadors received word that Sellier, the man who accompanied Courtenay to Fotheringhay Castle, reported that Courtenay had taken him into his confidence and told him that Paget had persuaded him to marry Elizabeth because if he did not, the Earl of Arundel would. Eight days later, Mary wrote a letter to the Princess of Portugal, Regent of Spain. The opening line immediately mentions her urgent need for money in order to survive. If there had been a more congenial opening of the letter, it was lost to either the decipherment or translation from Spanish. Regardless of the urgent need for money, Mary was able to continue with the preparations for Philip's arrival, which was growing closer. Philip was informed that his livery (for archers to wear) had arrived in England without any problems in a letter from the Ambassadors two days later. The Ambassadors also extended an invitation from the Queen for Philip to become a member of the Order of the Garter.

Renard informed the Emperor in a letter of 20 June on the progress of Courtenay's questioning. Courtenay had confessed that Hoby and Morison were directed by Paget, who had persuaded him marry Elizabeth, and he continued to declare that if it had not been for the influence they exerted on him that he (Courtenay) would not have proceeded as far as he did in the recent rebellion. Meanwhile, the Council received a proposal to send Elizabeth to the Court of the Queen Dowager of Hungary for a while, hoping Elizabeth would make friends, who would in turn inform the Council of anything Elizabeth might do or say.

On 26 June, news arrived in London that the Queen Dowager of Scotland was moving her forces of an estimated eight to ten thousand men to the border for the purpose of preventing the advancement of any rebels, but it was believed that her real objective was to give the disaffected English a chance to rise. It was also at about this time that several articles were drafted that outlined and described the services that were to be provided to Philip, amongst which was that a servant would be provided to translate both to and for Philip and to instruct him in basic English. His learning the language was of vital importance, and the speed at which he should learn it was strongly emphasized.

At some point in the month of July, John Christopherson wrote "*An Exhortation to all Menne to take hede of rebellion,*" an account of Wyatt's rebellion. This early account of the rebellion, with religious overtones, had mentioned that during the rebellion, "raping of virgins" had occurred, and included an account of Alexander the Greats' men raping virgins after conquering a city. Though there are only a few known accounts from that period, his is the only one that mentions such a reference to rape.

On 11 July, Prince Phillip set out for England aboard a Spanish Galleon, accompanied with what has been estimated at about sixty ships with between five thousand to seven thousand Spanish nobles, their servants, retainers, and livestock. Despite Renard's advice, gold bullion was also brought as a gift for the

English Treasury, and the French were kept clear so the Spanish fleet could sail unmolested. Mary's need for money did not affect the way she greeted the Marquess de Las Navas, who was given a gold chain adorned with rubies and topaz and with an agate on one side and a fiery diamond on the other. The Queen had also presented three chains to the men who accompanied the Marquess upon their arrival.

On 12 July, Juan Vasquez de Molian informed Francisco de Eraso that Philip would be sailing on a ship called La Brentandona, owned by Martin de Brentandona, and that Philip did board the ship that day hoping to have a wind in which they may cast their sail that evening. On 19 July, the Spanish fleet arrived at the Isle of Wight, and Philip quickly dispatched word of his arrival to the Queen. In the planning of Philip's arrival, it was at first believed that the harbor in the Isle of Wight could accommodate the fleet, but once all the ships where in the harbor, it was realized that there were too many people aboard too many ships for the small town to handle, and a decision was made to move the fleet to a larger harbor, Portsmouth, which was better able to handle the large group. Immediately upon hearing news, Renard dispatched a letter to the Emperor announcing Philip's arrival, and mentioned that Philip had arrived in port exactly one year to the day that Mary was proclaimed Queen.

The following day, before going ashore, Philip was presented with the insignia of the Order of the Garter and tied a garter around his leg. As Philip walked on English soil for the first time, artillery was fired and the Queen's minstrels played as Philip, accompanied by Renard, Courrieres, and others, made their way through the crowd. Philip then graciously received all those who came forward to kiss his hand, then mounted a caparisoned white hackney and proceeded on to Southampton, where they were greeted by English nobles and soldiers and attended a church where clergy performed a service. Then they departed on to the palace.

The following day, the Archbishop greeted Philip before attending mass, where it was noticed that Philip did not remove his hat. Philip was informed of the English custom, which he complied with immediately. After dinner he received the commission sent by the Queen, and expressed his gratitude towards her.

On the 23rd, Philip departed for Winchester after dinner in a heavy rainstorm. Upon his arrival, the Bishop and his clergy greeted him, and after changing his clothes, he made his way to the Queen, where a delighted crowd and the Queen with all her ladies received him. The following day after dinner, Philip returned to the Queen, escorted by the Queen's guard, along a passage filled with an assembly of English gentlemen and ladies. Philip visited the Queen for a long time, as he had done the day before. On St. James day, 25 July, the marriage ceremony that hundreds of people had perished trying to prevent took place.

Philip, accompanied by his nobles, who were adorned in gold and silver, and the Queen, accompanied by Englishmen magnificently dressed, preceded separately to the church. After their arrival, Philip and Mary took their place on a platform under a dais that stood four steps higher than the main platform and proceeded with the marriage ceremony. After the ceremony, Mass was recited and the Kings-of-Arms then proclaimed the titles of King and Queen, first of England and France, then of Naples, Jerusalem, and Ireland. Next were the Prince and Princess of Spain, Archduke and Archduchess of Austria, the Duke and Duchess of Milan, Burgundy, and Brabant, and Count and Countess of Flanders and Tyrol. After the ceremony, the newlyweds adjourned to the Great Hall for a magnificent feast, with entertainment and music that lasted about 5 hours. After the banquet, the Bishops blessed the couple and the marriage bed, and then bowed out to leave Mary and her husband alone for the first time.

After spending the night at reading, the King and Queen went to Windsor the following day, where Philip was established as head of the Order of the Garter, and they made their offerings at church. That night they lodged at the castle, an ancient building once belonging to the Templar. The King and Queen stayed in Windsor until 11 August, when Philip received news that the French and seized Renty (?) and that the Emperor had left Brussels to join the battle. All the gentry who had accompanied Philip to England requested leave, though they where not gone long because the French had withdrawn.

A Spanish gentleman who accompanied Philip to England and was present at all the lavish ceremonies and other matters of state wrote to a gentleman friend of his living in Salamanca, a town about 100 miles Northwest of Madrid, on 17 August, and described the recent events as seen by himself of the Spanish-English affairs. This gentleman described the Queen as not at all beautiful, small and flabby but not quite fat, with a fair white complexion, without eyebrows, and dressed poorly. The gentleman continued on to describe the other women he had noticed as very poor dressers, with short skirts showing their knees when they walked and portraying themselves as immodest when they walked and even when seated. They were neither beautiful nor graceful when they were dancing, and no Spanish gentleman had taken any interest in them at all because they did not meet their standards. He continued that the English ate and drank a great deal, and that eighty to one hundred very fat sheep, a dozen beef cows, and a dozen and a half calves, poultry, deer, boars and rabbits were consumed daily. The English, he said, drank enough beer to fill the Valladolid River (a river that runs North of

Madrid). This gentleman informed his friend that the English hated the Spanish as much as they hated the devil and that they were constantly robbed in town, on the road, or anywhere the robbers could commit their crime, and a large group of English had robbed and beaten over fifty Spaniards and they seem to go unpunished. Though he portrays a rather dismal and even dangerous image, for the most part the English just tolerated the foreigner's presence in support of their Queen.

A different gentleman who also accompanied Philip to England wrote to someone in Salamanca with a similar observation on 2 October of the women that he had seen, and described them as so far from beautiful that they were downright ugly. He continued by relating that, in general, the English treated the Spanish like animals and they tried not to notice them, but the Spaniards did the same towards the English, and that once the Queen had her child they could return home and leave these dreadful people behind. He concluded, "These barbarous English heretics are void of soul or conscience and fear neither God nor his saints."

From 23 August to 28 September, the King and Queen stayed at Hampton Court, often regarded as a magnificent abode, where construction was began in 1514. (It was best known for its excellent drainage system and clean water supply, which were regarded as healthier than those at the royal palaces.) On 18 September, a physician examined Mary by her request and concluded that she appeared to be pregnant. This was joyful news that was quickly spread, and because it appeared that the kingdom now had an heir, the pressure was removed from Elizabeth and Courtenay. Dispatches were quickly sent to inform the foreign Courts of this event, orders were issued to give public thanks, and great rejoicings were made as they assured themselves that the child would be a male. The news of Mary's pregnancy pacified the concerns of many, but there was still plenty that caused problems for the Spanish.

As events in England continued to quiet down and the English and Spanish tolerated each other better, Renard took advantage of the lull by requesting pay that was owed him for the past eight months, as well as reimbursement for the additional expenses that he had occurred out of his own pocket. In the beginning of November, Mary sent the Lord Paget and Edward Hastings, both members of the Privy Council, to Flanders, first to visit with the Emperor, and then to escort Cardinal Pole to England.

Parliament opened on 12 November. Before Mass, the King, riding a horse, and the Queen, riding in an open litter, both wearing their royal robes adorned with spotted ermine, made their way through the streets crowded with twenty thousand excited people towards the church of Westminster. Following Mass, the gathering made its way to the Parliament house, and the speaker of the House of Commons began with a two-hour speech. So began a long session of Parliament, with many important issues to address in front of a larger assembly than any other session. Renard wrote to the Emperor on 6 November with updates in the kingdom, and the most important other than Parliament was that everyone was sure that the Queen was pregnant. Renard noted that Mary's stomach clearly showed her with a child and that her dresses no longer fit.

A week had passed with Parliament discussing issues, such as a proposal to crown Philip, and trouble was brewing in Italy as the French were raising troops there. Suspicions rose that Elizabeth's relatives were again conspiring with the French. She was sick and had summoned the Queen's physicians, who had bled her to relieve a cold in her head. In the last week of November, Renard reaffirmed that the Queen continued to show signs that she was pregnant, and she had indicated that she felt the baby stir.

Cardinal Pole arrived in England on 24 November in the afternoon greeted by a few Lords and Bishops and friends and relatives. There was no ceremony for his arrival, but a cross was carried before him. Four days later, he addressed Parliament, and among the issues he discussed were his thanks for repealing the measure that banned him from England during the reign of King Henry VIII.

As much turmoil within the realm had settled down, and Elizabeth and Courtenay were in prison, the holiday season began. Mary had many things to celebrate this Christmas: she had a devoted husband, she was with his child and an heir to the kingdom, and the majority of those who caused her problems had been dealt with. Above all, her spirits were high and her health reflected it. The holiday celebrations began with cane play, tournaments, banquets, dancing, and masquerades. Many of the animosities between the English and Spanish had either been forgotten or set aside for the holiday season. On Christmas Eve, Pope Julius III blessed a small sword in a silver sheath with a cap that represented a dove woven into it, and sent the sword as a gift to Philip. Mary received a golden rose.

In the evening of New Year's Day of 1555, a group of Spaniards were discovered in the cloister of Westminster with a couple of prostitutes that caused an uproar, and a Spanish friar rang the church bells, sounding the alarm. The dean's men quickly responded to the alarm to find the entryway to the cloister guarded by Spaniards banishing pistols that fired and wounded some of the dean's men. The Spaniards were quickly apprehended, and the town returned to quiet before morning. The holiday season quickly ended as an act of Parliament commenced at the beginning of February that would deal harshly with heretics, and several where burnt at the stake, including the Bishop of Gloucester. The people of London were beginning to complain about the harsh treatment that Parliament had placed into effect.

Renard informed the Emperor that he received information that the French Ambassador's brother had been conspiring with Elizabeth, and followers of Courtenay had indicated that the French were helping to win the legate and Chancellor and secure their support in freeing Courtenay by any means. Renard warned the King and members of the Council, and spoke to the legate about the issue. Many were arrested who had been holding meetings praying for Elizabeth's release, and various forms of letters had been discovered reflecting the same.

Discussion of sending Elizabeth anywhere but within the kingdom had continued, and Renard informed the Emperor in a letter of 27 March that Courtenay had met with the Queen and begged her to pardon him. He promised to serve the Queen and the Emperor in whatever place he may have been told to go to if they granted his request for freedom.

CHAPTER 5. APRIL 1555 TO SEPTEMBER 1556. FREE-DOM AND SUSPICION

The exact date of Courtenay's release is not clear, but a letter of 8 April is the first to mention his release from Fodringham castle. Immediately after his release, he departed to pay his respects by going to Court to kiss the hands of his majesties. Courtenay again promised that he would go anywhere that the King and Queen might send him, and that he would marry anyone they wished.

Renard reported to the Emperor that several adversaries of the Chancellor had stated that he was instrumental in securing Courtenay's release, hoping to promote him to the crown if the Queen should die. Others have indicated that the legate Pole insisted on his release. Most felt that his release was too soon because he was "lightheaded and may easily lend an ear to further temptation." Releasing Courtenay did cause a problem, and releasing him without releasing Elizabeth could cause a riot. Therefore, the King and Queen decided to release other prisoners who were convicted of lesser crimes, and the Council proposed that Elizabeth should be released also. It was also proposed that

Courtenay should marry the widow of the Duke of Suffolk, Frances, mother of Lady Jane Grey, who came next after Mary, Queen of Scots, in the order of succession in line for the crown.

Courtenay was only concerned about his freedom, and he was soon preparing for his trip to Italy. On 29 April, he was informed that his request for carts and horses with several additional relief horses had been granted, and a servant of Thomas Martin sent them. Several additional horses were also sent for a Spanish friar that was perhaps rather large, as the Council and Lord Chancellor were amused at the additional request. Martin had sent several letters of reference to various merchants that would help Courtenay acquire supplies that he would need for his journey.

The following week, Renard informed the Emperor that Courtenay was going to Italy and wished to stop and pay his respects. Perhaps reflective of many people's opinions, Renard mentions that with Courtenay out of England, one of the many embarrassments is now out of the way. James Basset informed Courtenay that word had already been sent to the Emperor that if Courtenay arrived before the Duke of Alva departed on his journey that the Duke would present him to the Emperor upon his (the Duke's) arrival and Courtenay should be given as much honor as could be given. Basset concluded his letter by informing Courtenay that he had never seen the Queen so healthy and look as well as she did then.

There is some discrepancy about the day that Courtenay arrived in Calais, as several dates seem to exist. It is generally believed that Courtenay arrived in Calais on 8 May, but James Basset, while he was in London, wrote to Courtenay on 3 May in Calais thanking him for his gift of a great horse and informed him that King Philip had requested that the Duke of Alva present him to the Emperor. While Thomas Martin was in London he wrote to Courtenay on 29 April, but no address is given for Courtenay. It would be safe to speculate based upon that evidence that Courtenay had in fact arrived in Calais prior to 3 May.

On 8 May, Courtenay also wrote to Mr. Englefield and James Basset indicating that he had signed and placed his seal on a document pertaining to the sale on a manor of his. Though there is no name given about the manor, Courtenay described the estate as having two hundred acres, and which contained a large amount of timber and other commodities. Courtenay gave his approval for an appraisal to be taken and the worth of the estate to be determined as soon as possible. He may have anticipated a need for additional money to travel on in the future and decided to dispose of some property that had little meaning to him.

On the same day, Courtenay had written to his mother informing her that he had arrived in Calais, a town about one hundred miles north of Paris, safely, and that he would continue his journey the following day for Flanders, Belgium. Courtenay also wrote to the Lady Barkley thanking her for her letter, and that he was sorry whenever he thought of her broken bow. Courtenay also received a thousand crowns from Mr. Gresham and desired that his thanks be passed along through Mr. Englefield. Two days later, it was reported that the Earl of Pembroke had crossed the channel and was also at Calais, but several individuals indicated that he was unfit for the assignment because he could not communicate in any language but English.

On 15 May, the Marchioness of Exeter wrote a short note to her son while she was in Wallsanger and staying at the master Coram's house. The countess informed him that she received his letters of 8 May and 15 May, and that she would not rest until he had completed his journey by sea. Sir John Mason mentioned in a letter to Sir William Petre that Courtenay arrived in Brussels on Thursday, 16 May, but it was not until the 19th that Courtenay was escorted to the Emperor by the Duke of Alva, with the Duke of Chamberlain acting as his interpreter if Courtenay required one.

It was reported to John Mason that Courtenay had conducted himself very humbly to the Emperor. For almost a year and a half, the Emperor's ambassadors in England were constantly updating the Emperor with Courtenay's actions; it would be safe to assume that Courtenay had met several with mixed and diverse opinions about him. Regardless of any prejudices that may have been present, Courtenay conducted his business with respect and care that the King and Queen would hope for in these situations.

Courtenay expressed his gratitude to King Philip for helping him gain the Queen's favor and finally allowing him the opportunity to travel and better himself through those experiences, and offered his services to the Emperor. The Emperor expressed his interest in Courtenay's offer and responded that he may call upon him from time to time. Thrilled at his prospects with the Emperor, Courtenay explained that he was motivated not only by the desires of the King and Queen, but for his father, with whom the Emperor was familiar. The Emperor, wishing to show his approval, informed Courtenay that he should enjoy all that his Court had to offer.

Frederico Badoer, the Venetian Ambassador, reported that Courtenay arrived in Brussels on 17 May, and the Emperor assigned him lodging for the duration of his visit. The Emperor granted the Earl of Bedford's request to travel to Italy, but Courtenay's request would have to wait. James Basset wrote to Courtenay to inform him that, though he had tried, he was unable to obtain permission for his uncle John Blunt to travel and that it was perhaps best that he did not. Furthermore, Basset told Courtenay, the lands he wanted to sell had been entailed and Mr.

Heydon had sent the necessary documents for Courtenay to sign, but there were other matters regarding the sale. Basset was unable to mention them due to the limited time available for writing the letter. Basset recommended that Courtenay have a survey done to insure that the sale was fair for both parties. Basset also told Courtenay to review the assessment and to return it as his time allowed. Mr. Heydon had paid rent for a half of a year to Mr. Basset, who told Courtenay that the money was used to pay a couple of debts in England, with the remainder to be distributed in partial fulfillment of other debts. Other news that Basset passed along was that Cardinal Pole, the Chancellor, and the Lord Steward, had crossed the channel safely for Calais, and that Elizabeth was given her liberty but she remained at Court.

Two days later, Courtenay wrote several letters describing his interview with the Emperor. He wrote to the King and Queen in Italian and to Bernard de Fresnoda, the King's confessor, in Latin. He also wrote to the Chancellor and James Basset. On 20 May 1555, Courtenay wrote to Queen Mary:

> The Earl of Devon to the Queen,
>
> It may please your most excellent majesty to be advertised,
>
> On Sunday last, being the 19th of his month, the Duke of Alva brought me to the Emperor's majesty's presence; unto the which I delivered your majesty's letters, and therewithal offered my humble service. Of whose majesty the same was received even accordingly to the honorable and good nature of his highness, and as appertained to the letter of recommendation written from your majesty. For the which benefit and goodness of your grace, I think not myself less bounded to the same, albeit I have received both very many and most great; so that not only by service I am not able to acquit the same, but also I cannot by words express the due and humble thanks that I owe unto your majesty: so that this only resteth in my power that I shall not cease to pray almighty God to preserve not only to mine, but generally to the benefit of all Christendom, both your majesty and the Emperor's majesty; whom, greatly to my comfort, I was sitting up in his chair in such a case as it appeared his highness had both ease and convenient health of his person. Thus now I leave to trouble your

highness further, remaining most humbly at your majesty's commandment.

The 20th of May 1555 from Brussels.

Your majesty's most humble subject at commandment. [Tytler, pg.
474-475]

The Venetian Ambassador Badoer declared on 26 May that
he had received word that Courtenay had been approached with
the proposition of taking the Duchess of Lorraine as his wife
because the Duke of Savoy would not have her. Courtenay
declined due to his busy agenda. Three days later, Courtenay
wrote many letters while he was in Brussels. In the majority of
his letters, he only described his interview with the Emperor. In
his letter to Mr. Englefield, Courtenay mentioned that there was
no new news to report, but he quotes a proverb of the time that
"great Princes make peace with sword in hand," and even though
great persons were declaring peace, both sides were preparing
for the event of war. Courtenay was referring to the peace negotiations that were going on between France, England, and Spain,
which would also serve as a perfect learning opportunity for
Courtenay to expand his statesmanship and to understand how
to use the basic tools of ambassadorship. In a letter to his mother,
he only described his interview with the Emperor, and in the
remainder of those letters, he only thanks them for their
friendship. Courtenay informed James Basset that he had
requested permission to travel to Italy from the King, and he
complained about a problem that he had with his hip.

The Ambassador Don Ruy Gomez had dispatched a letter
updating the Emperor on the progress of the treaty, and meanwhile the French and English commissioners met at the house of
the Cardinal legate to discuss their issues towards peace. Each
side, having voiced their concerns, was unable to proceed any
farther. The Venetian Ambassador Frederico Badoer had mentioned in a letter that the Duke of Brunswick had dispatched

captains to raise troops and that the Saxon cavalry was recruiting in Philip's name. The commissioners met for four straight days that were filled with long debates, but remained at an impasse.

It was reported to the Venetian Bailo, who was at Constantinople on 12 June, that Pope Marcellus the Second had died after a long illness and that the Cardinal of Chieti, a member of the Caraffa family, had been appointed to replace him.

Courtenay wanted to go to Liege, a province in East Belgium, or Aquissgranda (West Germany?) to allow his hip to heal. James Basset responded to Courtenay's request for a leave of absence because of hip on 13 June by chastising Courtenay for considering leaving and saying that he should understand the King and Queen's desire for him to remain. It was conveyed to Basset through Ruy Gomez that King Philip expressed his strong desire for Courtenay to remain with the Emperor and that the Queen had concurred with Philip on the matter. It was also pointed out to Courtenay that doing anything different would most likely arouse suspicions. Basset concluded his letter by mentioning that he agreed with the King and Queen, and that he should stay where he was. Two days later the Cardinal Pole informed the Pope that the peace negotiations between France and England still had no conclusion and desired that the Pope make certain recommendations on the matter. Pole concluded that it was clear that both sides wished to continue with talks, but for now they had separated and Pole was going to return to England.

In early June, Sir John Mason had introduced Courtenay to Frederico Badoer, to whom Courtenay had expressed his desire to reside in Venice. Badoer had remarked in cipher what Courtenay had disclosed in the course of a conversation, "that he was evidently in great fear for his life, and thought of nothing but preserving it: though he had no suspicion of the Emperor, whose audience of him had been loving." A couple of days later, the Emperor had displayed affection to Lord Paget's son and son-in-law upon their arrival in Brussels by sending them refreshments, and this compliment had not been sent to Courtenay when he arrived. As the English had remarked, Courtenay was "infinitely superior" to the Paget's. Courtenay, with his wounded pride, departed Brussels to Lorraine in northwest France to visit with Mr. Bonvise, who had promised to advance him some credit with a recommendation from James Basset. This is the first indication that Courtenay was having money issues.

Rumors of Mary's pregnancy continued, but Ruy Gomez felt that the Queen was not pregnant at all, only pretending to be to keep Philip there and not allowing him to leave England to go to the Emperor and assist him with settling matters there. Renard had mentioned in a letter to the Emperor on 24 June that he had heard of a possible conspiracy in which Mary was not pregnant, and a suitable baby was sought to fill the role. Renard believed that this rumor was the product of the heretics.

The peace commissioners continued to meet and had several long sessions where the English delegates, the Earl of Arundel, the legate, the Chancellor, and Lord Paget, had been working diligently to arrive at anything that would be agreeable with the French. With each passing day that the peace negations stalled, both sides prepared for the possibility of war. In the last week of June, Courtenay wrote to Henry Neville, Lord Abergavenny, who served with her majesties' forces during the Wyatt rebellion, requesting he acquire some bucks and does for him to hunt. He said that he wished he could come to visit him but hoped to see him in England again soon, ready to again serve her majesties forces if England and France went to war.

The Venetian Ambassador in England reported that he had heard that the Scots had assembled troops along the border, and recommended to the Queen's Council to prepare for an attack from the Scots as a precaution. He also mentioned a desire for the Bishop of Arras to induce the Emperor to allow Courtenay to travel to Italy, who was very upset at not being allowed to go.

Rumors of Mary's pregnancy continued to flourish. Giacomo Soranzo, the Venetian Ambassador in France, reported on 30 June that when Cardinal Pole was asked about the Queen being pregnant, he replied with a laugh, "I know not whether she be or be not pregnant." Mary's physicians had originally indicated that she would deliver on 6 June, but they changed the date, stating that they made an error on judging the size of the fetus. There was again suspicion that she was not pregnant and was only trying to keep Philip from leaving England. Philip was most certainly having a difficult time choosing between his loyalties.

On the same day, Courtenay wrote to James Basset, telling him how honored he was by a visit from the Bishop of Arras at his house who only came to give his best wishes. The correspondence from Courtenay in the beginning of July reflected his need for money, as he requested an advancement to make some purchases, including a certain quantity of black velvet so he could make a nightgown. He began his letter to his mother describing his pleasurable experiences while he was in Brussels, where the Emperor, the French Queen, and the Duchess of Lorraine resided for most of the time, his purse was beginning to get light, hinting for her to send him some money.

In a letter to Dr. Martin, Courtenay thanked him for the letters he had sent, and he included a drawing of the fortifications at Brussels, though there are no further communications as to Martin's need for that information. There is no available information about the possibility of an attack there or that an attack or anything else had occurred or been planned at or shortly after that period of time.

Upon leaving Calais, Cardinal Pole wrote to the Pope on 6 July informing him of the progress he had made with his task of outlining, regulating, and reestablishing the hospitals, monasteries, and other churches with as little offense to the crown as possible. He also updated him with the status of the peace talks and said that the conference had been suspended without any further progress made, but both sides had expressed their desire to resume. Quite possibly as a result of the close of the peace negotiations, Courtenay had expressed his desire to further his travels, and on 8 July, Thomas Martin responded to Courtenay's desire to travel further by recommending that he remain in the low countries until King Philip arrived, and while he was waiting he should acquaint himself with the Bishop of Arras. Two days later, the Venetian Ambassador in France reported that peace talks had resumed but continued to remain at an impasse, and news that England was preparing ships for Philip's passage to Flanders. However, the French did not believe that the ships were for Philip but were preparing them to launch a war against them. The Duke of Alva recommended to the Emperor that the French should know the hope and promise of peace offered by Queen Mary, and that thirty thousand infantry and ten thousand horse soldiers would take the field in Flanders in an attempt to divert the war from Italy if required.

James Basset was pleased to hear that the Bishop of Arras treated Courtenay well in a letter to him on 12 July. Basset reminded Courtenay that having such an ally as the Bishop would only help him in the future and was glad that it worked to Courtenay's advantage. During the forth week of July, Courtenay's need for money had turned to desperation as he mentioned his strong need for money in various letters. Courtenay had also been in communication with several gen- tlemen in England who were handling several of his estates, and he informed the same gentlemen that the rumors that they heard that he was being held prisoner were false. Courtenay's request for money was granted shortly afterwards, as he finally received some relief in the form of one thousand crowns, which had been sent by Mr. Bonvise.

On 3 August, Courtenay informed a Mr. Gresham that he had departed Brussels and had arrived at Malines (Mechelen), a town about fifteen miles north of Brussels on his way to Antwerp, but he had to return to Brussels. The reason for his return to Brussels is revealed when the Venetian Ambassador Badoer, who was with the Emperor at the time, reported in a letter of 4 August that a servant of Courtenay had been mortally wounded by a Spaniard. The Ambassador continued that on two other occasions, twelve other Spaniards had picked quarrels with Courtenay's servants, and the Spaniards had even pursued them to their lodgings. There is no known reason for the Spaniard's behavior, other than they probably sought to repay the treatment they had received at some point during their stay in England. The Ambassador feared that the English would seek revenge if word were to leak out of the incident. The Bishop of Arras quickly dispatched word to the Queen and requested that those responsible be punished. Philip had also requested that the Bishop of Arras inform the Emperor and the Queen Dowager of Hungary about Courtenay's treatment. Philip also requested that Courtenay be treated well in the Low Countries so he may proceed to his next assignment safely. Perhaps in a gesture of goodwill, and to alleviate any concerns that Courtenay may have had regarding his safety, the Duke of Ferrara had dispatched his secretary to visit with Courtenay and invited him to remain for a while in his territory while Courtenay traveled to Italy.

It was discovered that a servant of the Lord Paget had returned to Italy from France pretending to be an Englishman with an excellent command of the language, and he was arrested on suspicion of being a spy. The Venetian Ambassador had reported to Venice that the Emperor could no longer trust Paget, and that Paget had written several letters to a friend in Venice indicating that Mary was not pregnant. Upon his return to Brussels, Courtenay had received a couple of letters from his mother, who updated him with the events in England and giving advice to avoid all sinful company. He had also received letters from a couple of gentlemen pledging their services to him, including Sir William Petre, who indicated that he would do him any service at Court. To use on his journeys, Courtenay had received some horses a few weeks prior and was now expecting some more from England, which were to come to him by way of Calais, and Courtenay requested that the Lord Wentworth ensure that they be allowed to pass without problem, as they were needed at once.

Preparations for Philip's departure continued, and Cardinal Pole informed the Pope on 28 August that the King and Queen had dined in London. Afterwards they went to Greenwich, where crowds celebrating St. Bartholomew's fair applauded them through their journey until they departed from the Tower wharf. The Venetian Ambassador Giovanni Michiel described that the fleet that would take Philip across the channel had consisted of twelve ships and a galleon, which were heavily armed and would sail with Philip and guard against any possible attacks by the French.

On 29 August, the King left the Queen and most of his household in the charge of Don Diego de Acevedo, his master of the household, and departed to Canterbury and then to Dover, where he would then cross the channel with the intent to return to the Queen sometime in October. During the first week of September, Courtenay received information that the King and Queen were upset with the treatment that he received earlier in Brussels, and the King indicated that he would see Courtenay on his trip to Flanders and assured him that recommendations had been made for his safe passage. When Courtenay received information that Philip was coming to Calais, he departed Brussels to greet him. As he rode through Brussels, some Spaniards, presumably because of some former dispute, attacked his attendants. As he reproved the assailants, he was answered by more threats, and as he noticed that more of their countrymen were on the way to assist, he fled to his lodging. On his retreat, four of his attendants were wounded, but some of the Spaniards had been also. Courtenay immediately reported the incident to the Bishop of Arras, and complained that it was now the forth assault that he and his attendants had suffered. The Bishop had assured him that these annoyances would not occur again.

On 4 September, Philip arrived in Calais, where the Emperor's troops and the president of the Emperor's chamber greeted him. Accounts at Lille reported that Philip arrived safely from England between five and six o'clock in good spirits and greeted everyone while holding his cap in one hand. From there Philip would depart to meet the Emperor in Brussels. As King Philip and Ruy Gomez set out from Calais, Courtenay and John Mason rode out to meet them on 8 September at the Casino near the gate into Lorraine. Upon their arrival, the King knelt before his father and attempted to kiss his hand, but the Emperor would not allow him to do so and Philip instead kissed his arm. Then Philip introduced the Admiral, Lord William Howard, and the Earls of Arundel and Pembroke to the Emperor, who greeted them properly but would not allow them to kiss his hand because they were not his own subjects.

In the third week of September, Sir Englefield informed Courtenay that his traveling to Italy had been proposed to the King and Queen, but with the King now traveling and the Queen unable to come to a decision without him, it would be addressed again later. On 18 September, the funeral ceremonies for Queen Joan of Spain, the Emperor's mother, concluded, and a rich and lavish banquet was planned in which the Queen Dowager of Hungary would feast with the King of England at Terueren with his Lords accompanying him. The following day, news arrived in Brussels that the new Pope, Giampietro Carafa, or Paul IV, was raising troops against the Emperor under the pretext that the Emperor had seized two French galleys on imperial territory. Philip wrote a sharp letter to him regarding his actions and informed him that no French ships were taken.

As rumors spread that Mary was not pregnant, discussions were now more frequent about the consort being given to Eliz- abeth, the next heir if the King and Queen did not have a child. Many nobles in England had thought, and a few had attempted, to marry their sons to Elizabeth with an eye on the crown. The Ambassador to the King of the Romans, who was with the Emperor, indicated that Courtenay, who was with him in Brussels, said that Courtenay had no interest in marrying the Lady Elizabeth and felt that she would not accept him anyway. Several other matches were considered for Elizabeth, including Prince Ferdinand and the younger son of the King of the Romans. It was also suggested to wait five or six years for Don Carlos to mature and the present King and Queen could reign undisturbed. Finally, the Duke of Savoy was also considered a worthy match.

Courtenay wrote to Englefield with a mysterious tone describing that he was unable to disclose what was on his mind regarding recent matters and that he was very busy, in a letter of 25 September. Certainly with Philip present and the tensions surrounding the stalled peace talks, and as rumors of both sides raising armies continued, Courtenay was both very busy and very prudent, too wary to disclose his preoccupations in a letter, whether in cipher or not, because someone may intercept it, like the French. Though the peace negotiations were the main and only real news, there was not a lot to report, and all correspondence reflected it for this short period. Courtenay did not correspond much during September, most likely for those reasons.

Shortly before 13 October, King Philip informed Mary that he was unable to return to England because of important issues that must be addressed while he was with the Emperor. Federico Badoer had reported that Philip felt that by staying in England, he was required to address issues that were unfit for his dignity. As ruler of Spain, he ruled absolutely in all things, and it was strange to him to share with the Council and other members of the English government. Philip also informed the Queen that he expected that the Englishmen who had plundered and ransacked the house of a certain Spaniard to be punished. It was believed that the Englishmen did so in revenge for the assaults of Courtenay's servants.

Mary was able to continue with the punishment of other heretics regardless of Philip's presence, and on 16 October, the Bishop of London (Ridley) and Latimer Bishop of Worcester were burnt at the stake in front of a large crowd.

On 17 October, Englefield informed Courtenay of the results of the surveys of some of the lands that he wished to sell, and of the discovery of several obsolete and hidden rents that may be of some help. Courtenay had also informed Sir William Petre that he had obtained permission from King Philip to travel, and he wrote to the Queen on 22 October requesting that his service be extended to travel farther abroad. He made similar requests to Cardinal Pole and the Lord Chancellor, who was rumored to be seriously ill. Hearing that Courtenay would most likely be given permission to continue his travels, Thomas Harvey informed him that he would welcome the opportunity to travel with the Earl.

With the usual ceremonies, Queen Mary opened a session of Parliament in Greenwich on 21 October, in which she sat on a well-decorated throne on top of a platform as she had at a previous session. Though the King was not present this time, the Queen was accompanied by most of the Lords, Barons, and other prelates, all wearing the attire suited to the occasion. In addition to those nobles, the Legate Pole was also present at the request of the Queen. The next couple of days were spent electing and confirming the speaker, and then addressing the motions and resolutions to be made. The Venetian Ambassador reported that Philip had received word from the Queen that several violent opposition members had returned to Parliament. Among the issues was Philip's coronation; Philip wanted the crown but they would not allow it. The Queen requested his return to address the issue. If he could not, then she would allow them to decide.

The Ambassador also reported that the wife of Peter Carew had come from England to visit with the King on 27 October. She was accused of leading a group of followers who were going to "cut the Spaniards to pieces" on the night before Philip was to leave England. She requested that her husband, who at that time was in Antwerp, be allowed to return to England, and that Philip pass along a kind word to the Queen regarding the matter or her husband would enter the service with the King of France. Philip considered several things before he finally informed her that he would give his recommendation to the Queen about her husband.

On the same day, James Basset informed Courtenay in a letter of the progress with the surveys of his lands, and of Mr.

Peter (Sir William Petre, Secretary of State), who had again indicated that he was interested in purchasing the manor of Whiteford. His assessment of the property noted discrepancies in the size and position of the property in relation to the manor of Shute that used to belong to the Duke of Suffolk. Basset concluded that he believed that this session of Parliament would be short. On 28 October, two men were hanged in Fleet Street for the crime of robbing a Spaniard that had occurred earlier in the month. It was believed that the Englishmen did so as retaliation against the attack on Courtenay's servants, and that they were executed by word from Philip.

Plagued by further depleting supply of money, Courtenay informed Sir William Petre that he would consider selling his manor of Whiteford to him in a letter of 2 November. Courtenay then informed Sir Walgrave, James Basset, and his trustees that he authorized them to sell the manor of Whitford in Devon to Sir William Petre, and included directions for conducting the transfer. In concluding his letter, Courtenay informed Mr. Basset that he had taken leave of the Emperor and the King, who had written him letters to use as an introduction upon arriving at various locations and when meeting with Ambassadors during his future travels. Courtenay mentions to Mr. Basset his now urgent need for money so he could begin his travels. He also urged Englefield to make haste with the transaction of his manor of Whitford. The Queen had asked Mr. Basset to pass along her desire to see Courtenay in England before he was to travel farther away. On this, Courtenay made a request to return to England for a short visit as the Queen had requested, but he found that his request was not well taken by the members of the Council, who recommended against his return for any reason, whether it be short or long. Many still believed that they had rid themselves of a nuisance to the kingdom and that he was better off where he was, rather than in England. This opinion prevailed and prevented him from returning to England to visit his mother, who was now ill and wrote him with great difficulty in the first week of November.

Courtenay had to make reductions in his staffing as a result of the shortage of funds, and informed Sir Thomas Tresham and John Trelawny that he was releasing their sons from his service. This was due only to financial concerns and not as a result of poor service from their sons. Then he departed Brussels on 7 November to travel through Germany to Italy. On 11 November, the Venetian Ambassador mentioned in his letter that Courtenay had requested that Don Ruy Gomez persuade King Philip to allow him to travel to England to sell some of his estates to help with the cost of his trip to Italy. Philip did not grant his request, but the King gave him several additional letters of recommendation to use while in the provinces. Courtenay departed rather discouraged with only four horses, and on 12 November, he arrived in Lorraine in Northwest France, and dispatched several letters in which his bitterness for not being able to visit England was prevalent and had a tone of desperation. His need for money had now pushed him to have William Petre address the Queen of his condition. He also wrote to several others requesting money, and to James Basset with directions on how to dismiss his servants in England. Courtenay also sent directions to William Petre on sending him forty barrels of beer for his household servants.

Courtenay had indicated that when he eventually departed from Lorraine, he would accompany the Elector as far as Cologne, where they would part, and Courtenay would continue with "great haste" to Mantua, then to Ferrara, and maybe visit Milan before going to Venice. Shortly after his pleas for money were sent, Courtenay mentioned his meeting with Peter Carew in Antwerp as a positive one, as he found Carew was willing to serve the King and Queen, though his religious views were unchanged and still influenced him a great deal.

On 13 November, news arrived that the Lord Chancellor, a friend who quite possibly saved Courtenay more than once and was instrumental in his release, died from what was at first believed to be from poison. An autopsy later determined that he died from dropsy, and he was buried in the church where he served as Bishop, leaving behind a small estate.

Parliament was continuing its session, and though they were divided in regards to the Chancellor, as some felt that his loyalty was more to the cause of the heretics, they were all saddened by his death.

Regardless of their personal feelings, the session yielded the passing of several bills, including the implementation of a subsidy tax to help the economy and a bill prohibiting the assembly and meetings of persons for the purpose of card playing and dice. A bill was also proposed that would prohibit the exportation of beer and grain.

The Venetian Ambassador Frederico Badoer wrote in a letter that King Philip's attendants said that he would return to England when the Emperor departed for Spain. An unknown source informed the Venetian Ambassador that the Emperor wanted Philip to return only for a few weeks, enough time for him to satisfy the Queen's wishes and to promote the thought of making war with France, although he could not say if this was a reliable source of not.

Sir Philip Hoby a noted diplomat, informed Courtenay in a letter of 20 November that bad weather had prevented him from meeting him in Lorraine and that he would meet him in Antwerp. Hoby asked Courtenay to consider the young Sheldon for an apprenticeship of sort, were Courtenay could direct and encourage his studies, and concluded that he would not mention the death of the Chancellor because it might further upset Courtenay. Courtenay replied to Hoby on 21 November that he was pleased that he was allowed to travel to Lorraine and that he hoped to visit with him in Antwerp before he departed. Courtenay is rather enigmatic in his letter at this point, perhaps for security reasons:

> The lets shall be very great, and my business very extreme, but we will have both our desires satisfied, for I have also somewhat to do with Mr. G. bis; but keep it very secret, for if I perform it (as I would you should not too assuredly look for it) I will so steal on you as no unnecessary man shall be privy thereunto, neither going, coming nor remaining there. [Brown, 254]

Rawdon Brown, who undertook the rather monumental task of deciphering, translating, and assembling the letters and documents in his *Calendar of State Papers and Manuscripts*, has indicated that the words "Mr. G. bis" may be read as "No 4 bis" or "Mr. G. bis" and attributes the discrepancy to cipher that could not be decoded and could refer to a deal that Courtenay was working on with Gresham in Antwerp. Courtenay concluded his letter by indicating that he would be happy to help the young Sheldon with his studies and would look for him to arrive soon, as he had not yet arrived.

James Basset informed Courtenay of the financial matters that he was handling on his behalf. After Basset received word that Courtenay could not come to England, Basset quickly requested advice on how to proceed with the deal that Courtenay had made with Gresham without harm to Courtenay. He would not proceed with so weighty of a matter on his own without Courtenay's guidance. Basset further explained to Courtenay that the way he had chosen to raise money would be disastrous and would ruin him if he proceeded, and that he should do business with the Lucchese banker Buonvisi, whose reputation was one of honesty and integrity. Basset informed

Courtenay that he should request credit in the amount of six thousand ducats to pay his bills and his trustees, and to only request what was required and no more. Basset had delivered one thousand pounds (English) to Courtenay for his travels and to keep his appointments with Mr. Gresham and Mr. Bonvise. Basset told Courtenay that he would continue to seek sources in which his creditors in England could be satisfied, and he had dispatched a small amount of money to Blunt for Courtenay upon his arrival. It appears that this letter was delivered to Courtenay while he was in route to Liege and Cologne from Lorraine.

A couple of days later the Venetian Ambassador announced that Queen Mary had named the Bishop of Ely (Thomas Thirlby) the most worthy to fill the position of the Lord Chancellor, though Philip felt that Paget would be best suited for the position. While Philip was in Brussels, the Emperor, who had plans of retiring and was now satisfied with his son's abilities, and with the approval of his Council, had renounced all his realms, provinces, countries, and Lordships in favor of his son without holding back anything in Spain, Italy, or the Low Countries. The official seals were renewed and titles were confirmed just as if the Emperor died and the rightful heir succeeded. Don Diego de Acevedo had departed London by Philip's orders on Christmas Eve to cross the channel. During their journey, a sloop was lost with twenty of the King's mules and twenty-five people.

Peace negotiations continued with some progress now, and talk of releasing the prisoners were used to stall for time while a decision was made regarding the involvement of Queen Mary and Cardinal Pole to act as mediators. By the close of December, a break was agreed on with the understanding that both sides wished to continue.

Courtenay informed Marman Ryngk (Rink?) that he had arrived in Augsburg as of 29 December and had taken his advice in choosing a new guide, and had sent back the bearer, who was very trustworthy and diligent. Courtenay continued by informing him that his belongings had arrived at Mentz, where he met a gentleman that saw to every need, and he appreciated it a great deal as it made his journey better. Courtenay concluded his letter by mentioning that the plague was raging in Venice. By 15 January 1556, Peter Vannes received information that Courtenay had arrived in Padua, Italy, and invited him to come to Venice the following day, where a grand public ceremony was to be held. The Council of Ten proposed to narrate an apology to be passed along to Courtenay for not showing him an offer of their goodwill and esteem towards him, and would do so when the opportunity arose. They voted with twenty-three agreeing to the proposal and one against, with two undecided, on 8 February.

The following day, the Venetian Ambassador Soranzo, who was in France, announced that the French had finally arrived at a truce with England. The terms included that neither side was to give restitution of any kind, that the truce be valid in all of either King's realms' on both land and sea, and that it would commence on 5 February and last for five years. Philip adjusted the wording to include the Queen.

Responding to possible threats to either himself or his attendants, Courtenay petitioned the Council of Ten on 10 February for a license for both himself and fifteen servants to carry weapons in the city of Venice, and surrounding areas, which was granted by a unanimous vote. The following day, Courtenay requested an additional ten servants on the license, which was also granted unanimously.

On 13 February, a letter of patent from King Henry II of France was read in public which informed everyone of the new treaty and of its articles between the King of France, the Emperor, and King Philip of England, which would last for a period of five years. The Venetian Ambassador was informed that the Emperor had stepped aside in favor of his son Philip, who would now succeed in all honors and estates from his father, in a letter of 15 February. King Philip had also received the realms and signories of the crown of Castille and Aragon, in addition to those previously awarded by his father. This would now prevent Philip from returning to England for a while longer. On the same day, an introduction of Courtenay was delivered to the Doge (the chief magistrate in the republics of Venice and Genoa) and Senate upon his arrival in Venice, which addressed the issue of his arrival and the matter of giving him a reception that cost one-hundred ducats that would cover refreshments and other things that were required.

On 22 February, William Rice, who was in London, wrote to Courtenay with updates in England. The most noteworthy at that time was the five-year truce between France and England. King Philip, who was still in Flanders, had solemnized the feast of "Toyson," and it would appear that his stay would be prolonged until after Easter. Courtenay's mother was seen more in Mary's court now and was in good health. Rice also included greetings to be passed along from several ladies and gentlewomen, including Anne Wharton, Lady Waldgrave, and Mrs. Bayman, who had lost her maidenhood since his departure.

By mid-March, a plot was discovered that involved robbing the exchequer and to capture the Queen, and by late March, most of those involved were in prison and questioned. As a precaution, the Queen was heavily guarded, but the ports were reopened and the ships were released, and couriers were now allowed to travel as required. A warrant was issued for James Crofts, who was regarded as one of the chief commanders in the kingdom and was part of Wyatt's rebellion. As a result of those actions, he was sentenced to death, but the Queen showed him leniency and released him. Sir Anthony Kingston, who several months earlier used sharp language during a session of Parliament that resulted in his imprisonment in the Tower, also received clemency by the Queen and was released. Interrogating the various prisoners had revealed that the main plot was not only to rob the exchequer and carry the rewards off, but also to murder the Queen in what has been called the "Dudley Conspiracy," because it was believed that Henry Dudley, brother of the late Duke of Northumberland, was among the leaders. Further questioning of the prisoners revealed that the whole had an understanding with some foreign Prince, but it is unclear who this was.

On 20 March, Philip wrote to his Ambassador in Venice,

> "I have seen what you say about Courtenay and the message he took to you. You will do well to watch him carefully and find out everything he is up to. If he leaves that place and proceeds towards Milan or Piedmont, you will immediately inform the Cardinal and the Marquess of Sarria and also let me know."

> [Tyler, C/D&SP, 259]

As the arrests continued, a man was arrested for having communicated with Courtenay, who had a servant, Walker, imprisoned on suspicion of his involvement in the recent conspiracy. Of course, with these two imprisoned, suspicion of Courtenay's involvement increased; after all, Courtenay had a great need for money and many knew that just by reading the letters to and from him. The Queen was greatly troubled by the recent incident, and she had also received news that Philip had further delayed his return as he prepared for the arrival of the King and Queen of Bohemia.

By 7 April, twelve more individuals were implicated, though not men of great importance, they were charged as rebels and traitors, as was Henry Dudley, who fled to France. In addition to other servants of Courtenay who were in prison, another servant, Stadan, regarded as a very meddlesome busybody, was also confined and heavily questioned. Further questioning of the prisoners revealed that the conspirators had intended to flee to the Isle of Wight, and many there were soon implicated with the recent incident, including the Captain of the Isle of Wight, who was released after finding nothing to tie him with the traitors. It was believed that, of the prisoners in the Tower, ten to twelve were expected to be executed after Easter.

By now Mary had received information regarding Philip's extended absence that rose suspicions, and she decided to send the Lord Paget under the pretence of congratulating the Emperor and the King on arriving at an agreement with France on a truce. But she was really sending him to report on Philip's real intentions for not wanting to return to England, and if his majesty was to wait for the arrival of the King and Queen of Bohemia, who would have to travel a long distance anyway, to travel a little further and come to England.

On 13 April, Paget arrived in Brussels and had numerous long conversations with the King, where they discussed his return to England and where he would be crowned, which still had not occurred. Philip indicated that ten to twelve days after the arrival of the King and Queen of Bohemia, he would return to England, where he would spend some time with the Queen before proceeding to Spain. Having Philip's assurance of his return, Paget presented letters to the Emperor with congratulations on his successful Ambassadorship.

The following day, the Venetian Ambassador in England reported that precautions had been taken on the Isle of Wight, which was well fortified with a garrison and guns. A register had been made of all able-bodied men in case of the necessity for arming, and all nobility and gentry had been placed on watch. The Ambassador also reported that a majority of the prisoners of the recent conspiracy had indicated, independently of one another, that they had intended to make Courtenay their king. The Ambassador had concluded by indicating that ten of the prisoners were men of quality.

Meanwhile in Brussels, Philip was addressing more important issues. He was practicing his jousting with various nobles in a private park with the intent of going public when the King and Queen of Bohemia arrived.

On 21 April, it was reported that Sir Anthony Kingston had died of "stone," which seized him while on his way to prison in London under heavy escort, apparently a more fortunate death than he would have experienced had his sentence been carried out. He had confessed to being part of the conspiracy not only to kill the Queen, but also to indiscriminately kill all foreigners. Further questioning of the prisoners revealed two men who were regarded as the ringleaders: John Throgmorton, who spent a great deal of time in Italy and Venice, and Thomas Uvedale, who was a keeper of one of the fortresses on the Isle of Wight. They were both declared traitors and sentenced to die on 28 April. They were first dragged behind horses through the city to their place of execution, where they were then hanged but not allowed to die. Then they were cut down their midsection and their entrails were removed and thrown on a fire at the base of the gallows, and afterwards they were quartered and their heads placed on the city gates.

The Venetian Ambassador Michiel in England informed the Doge and Senate in Venice that he had received information that Courtenay was invited to Ferrara by the Duke for the main reason of tempting and persuading him to depart from France to serve the King, who had promised him an honorable provision. Upon further investigation, it was revealed that Courtenay did in fact leave Venice to Ferrara on 21 March, where he remained for a period of four or five days before returning.

On 5 May, five more of the prisoners were sentenced because of their involvement: Sir John Paratt, Sir John Pallard, Sir Nicholas Arnold, Sir John Chichester, and Sir William Courtenay, a cousin of Edward Courtenay. All would serve their sentences in the fleet prison next to the Fleet River. William Courtenay had spoken with Throckmorton in private shortly before his execution, and just before Throckmorton's conference with the Dean of Westminster, John Feckenham. Feckenham reported that Throckmorton said nothing about the conversation he had with William Courtenay, but it was revealed that the plot was discovered by intercepted letters from Henry Dudley to John Throckmorton through a conference that Throckmorton had with Sir Edward Hastings, the Queen's master of the horse.

Arrests continued and twenty more were either confined in the Tower or sent to the fleet prison on the banks of the Fleet River, including several nobles, and some had served with Thomas Wyatt but were released due to a lack of evidence against them. By 19 May, three more were imprisoned and one was sentenced to death. Added to the list of prisoners was a widow who had fled and was later captured at seaside, most likely looking for a way to France. News had arrived from Flanders that Peter Carew, who escaped capture after Wyatt's rebellion, and Doctor Cheke, tutor of the late Edward VI, had been captured and would be brought to England. By the end of May, several more executions had taken place and more were imprisoned. Several depositions had been taken from those involved, including John Danyell and John Seyntlowe, and Edward Courtenay's name came up several times. To this point, there was not enough evidence against Courtenay to bring him back to England.

On 1 June, Carew and Cheke arrived from Flushing and were taken straight to the Tower under guard, though the matter was kept as secret as possible. Reports that the King of France was upset by their capture arrived shortly after. News also arrived at Court that Kilgrew was currently at sea with three ships funded by the King of France with the intention of enabling Elizabeth to escape from England.

By the beginning of July, the affairs of the conspiracy had settled down, and most of the main conspirators had been executed or imprisoned. The strict confinements of Sir William Courtenay, Carew, and Cheke had been reduced, and their wives were allowed to come and go as they pleased and had often spent the night with their husbands in the Tower. Most of the ships had been disarmed and released, with the exception of about seven that were kept ready for the King's passage.

Renard indicated in a letter in mid-July that the Queen had ordered Edward Courtenay to return to England and address the charges against him. Renard also mentioned that an Englishman by the name of Neville had returned to England from Venice and had mentioned that Courtenay had rented a house there. The Queen had received word through Ambassador Wotton that the French could no longer do anything for the rebels without provoking war and that they could no longer use Courtenay at any price. Philip had dispatched Andrew Tremayne to visit with Courtenay and to learn of any intrigues that he might be planning.

On 11 July, Courtenay wrote to the Lady Mason thanking her for a token that she had sent to him, and he sent a token to her son-in-law Cheke. This is recorded as being the last letter from Edward Courtenay, and no further correspondence is known to have survived. After Courtenay died, a large cache of his writings was discovered and many of those letters disappeared, never to read by anyone, possibly preventing their contents from ever being disclosed.

On 15 July, Mary wrote a rather nasty letter to the Emperor that was sarcastic in tone. She was upset that the Emperor had broken his promise in which he had told her that Philip would have returned by then, which he had not. Mary had also indicated that she was sending an emissary to Flanders to visit with the King and Queen of Bohemia. By 21 July, the Queen had again written to Courtenay, who was still in Venice, but this time to inform him that all the charges against him had been dismissed and that he was again in her favor, and the King had expressed his favor also.

On 27 July, the King and Queen of Bohemia arrived in Brussels, and the Emperor had arrived the day before. There was a great rush of people to Brussels to see the six crowned heads who where assembled there: the Emperor, King Philip, the King and Queen of Bohemia, Eleanor, Queen Dowager of France, and Maria, former Queen of Hungary. During their stay, there were several jousting tournaments, combats on foot, and feasts and banquets, some organized by the town and some by Court. The King and Queen stayed in Brussels until 15 August.

In the first week of August, forty more of the conspirators were hanged between the Isle of Wight and Portsmouth Harbor, and a few were executed in London. Some of the leaders had their execution delayed so they could be questioned more, hoping that the executions of their fellow conspirators would pressure them to disclose important information. During the same week, Philip, who was still in Brussels, dispatched news of the death of Lord Maltravers, the only son of the Earl of Arundel. Only twenty-two at the time of his death, he was the last descendent, and without an heir, the family name died when he did. Rumors that he died from poison were prevalent.

As the heretics were dealt with in England, trouble was brewing in Rome as the Pope was preparing for war against the

Emperor and Philip. King Henry II of France had informed the Pope that he would be ready and able to assist the Pope with ships and men-at-arms if required. On 15 August, the Venetian Ambassador in Rome reported that eight French galleys brought an estimated eighteen hundred men, who had assembled about twenty miles from Rome. A few days before, the Pope had told a small group of Roman cavaliers that several fortifications were in place and if they made any threats, the Pope's army would destroy them and that God would help them do so. The Pope had also threatened to deprive Philip of his crown.

Trouble was again brewing in England, and three days later it was reported that a man whose name was Cleobury had issued proclamations in various locations that Queen Mary had died. Among the locations was a church were Cleobury had proclaimed, "The Lady Elizabeth Queen and her beloved bed fellow Lord Edward Courtenay King." Cleobury indicated before his death that he had done this in Courtenay's name. Immediately those who were involved were captured and two of the leaders were executed, including the parish priest of the church where Cleobury made his proclamation. Twelve others that were involved had been captured and brought to the Tower, including Kilgrew and six or eight of his accomplices. By 21 August, interrogations of Peter Kilgrew revealed that he had indicated that he was to receive aid from France and his involvement with Dudley and others, and he confessed to fitting out and arming two ships and plundering a Spanish vessel and others at sea.

Mary was beginning to show signs of anxiety at the recent events in England, coupled with what was described as the hottest days that anyone could remember. As many believed that Philip was avoiding her on purpose, Mary traveled about eight miles to Croydon to stay in a house owned by the Legate Pole with the purpose to get away to recover her health. As Mary attempted to relax, reports came in during the last week of August about the leader of the last conspiracy, who was a French captain who would make a proclamation in a town sometimes disguised as a peasant, a wayfarer, or a merchant, and would wear a certain type of clothing one time and a different one another so he would not be recognized or tracked, and he would then disappear into the forests of England to hide. Orders had been given to capture him, and bloodhounds would be used to track and locate him should he appear again.

During the last week of August, Courtenay had traveled to Lio, a small piece of an island about six miles from Venice, to enjoy time watching his hawk fly around the wasteland, but he was suddenly overtaken by a storm that prevented him from returning to Venice by his gondola. He was forced to take a searcher's boat that had arrived at his location by chance, and drenched and refusing to change into dry clothes, he left for Venice.

On 6 September, the Venetian Ambassador in Rome reported that the first invasion of the Papal territory had occurred by the Imperialists. News arrived that Ascanio della Cornia had captured a large garrison, and another had surrendered. Such a panic had prevailed in the city that large quantities of people attempted to flee, but they were not allowed to pass the city gates. All able-bodied men were quickly summoned to guard the city as soldiers assembled to do the same. Soon enough men were mustered, and even though the Imperialists had made several successful attacks, they were repulsed, and many Spaniards were disarmed. Men from hundreds of miles left to defend Rome as the women and children fled for safety, as news arrived that the Imperialists had seized several small towns outside of Rome. News traveled quickly to Courtenay, who was only about two hundred and fifty miles away and chose to remain where he was instead of fleeing, as so many others were doing.

To avoid the plague, Peter Vannes had left Venice for Padua and had indicated that Courtenay informed him that he had fallen on the stairs of his house, but he did not feel any pain and traveled to Padua during the end of the first week or the beginning of the second week of September. To avoid the tedious and boring trip by water and to spare the horses, Courtenay decided to travel in what Vannes described as the worst possible way, which was by coach, which was bumpy and uncomfortable. He arrived in Padua on Saturday, 12 September. Peter Vannes indicated that he arrived the following day to find Courtenay very weak, and he grew worse over the next couple of days. Courtenay had refused visitation from anyone, including friends, and had now accepted two physicians that attended to him with great diligence. Courtenay quickly realized that his condition was growing worse, and he instructed his servants to take an inventory of all his small items and pay special attention that all his writings and letters there and in Venice should be put in order and await any royal orders regarding them. Vannes also realized that Courtenay would not recover, and began to plan his burial on a rather small budget with various local merchants, but still to give him the honors that he deserved. With the support of Queen Mary, he had a credit of three or four thousand crowns in which to work with. Vannes blamed Courtenay's improvised financial state on the lack of interest of the Council, and was irritated that they did not take the time to remember Courtenay with monetary payments.

On 18 September, Courtenay's health had only worsened, and he had received his communion and had answered in broken words that he accepted the church as a thing most necessary. In repentance of his sins, he opened his eyes and hit his chest with his fist. Vannes had Courtenay rest before the sacraments were read, and Courtenay forced himself to take communion, but his tongue had swollen and he clenched so hard that he was unable to proceed any further. He died shortly after on the same day.

A couple of weeks before Courtenay died, he confided in Vannes that many had told him since his arrival he was better French than English and that he would quarrel with his sword as soon as he recovered. Vannes wrote to the Queen after Courtenay's death requesting that his funeral expenses be paid and that his servants, of which there were ten and now master-less, money less, and not able to live there or be able to return to their homes.

There now remains very little correspondence to and from Courtenay during the last few months of his life, but prior to that time he had written many letters, sometimes six in just one week. Upon his death a large cache of his writings was discovered by the Council of Ten in Venice, and a certain number of these letters where removed from the box, never to be read by anyone. Vannes had indicated that Courtenay had chosen to lead a sol-itary life, only seeing a few close friends, but it is quite possible that Courtenay was involved in some intrigue that history has hidden in the shadow of the White Rose.

Chapter 6. Epilogue for Edward Courtenay

The following is the speech read in the temple of Antony, by Thomas Wilson of England, in Padua on 21 September 1556, upon the death of Edward Courtenay. This has been translated from the original Latin text:

> You see before you a funeral, solemn indeed, and a sad display: dust, not man; a corpse, not a person; trunk, not soul; a mass without mind, a vessel without liquid, a ring without a stone. It is a difficult thing, a dark transformation, a woeful event. You see a youth, not one among the many of the common crowd, but alone amongst the many and therefore, one of his kind: not such that few praised him, but whom all admired; not the kind of person whom only the common crowd favored, but the kind of person whom Princes would notice. I speak of a youth of noble birth, shining with dignity, with excellent character, abounding in a wealth of decorations of every kind.

> But what youth do I commemorate to you? An English youth, and one indeed who was most noble of the English. I speak of the youth Edward Courtenay, Earl of Devon, hope of his fatherland, pride of his country, ornament of Britain. I say in pain that he who was uplifted to the highest hope in enlarging and celebrating his dignity, now he lies, sunken, in the ground: consumed by illness, in a coffin and wrapped up in bandages. Oh! Heaven, oh gods above, oh slippery and uncertain race of ours, oh false hope, oh life's highest inconstancy. He whom so many Princes knew (Princes that no longer know him by his face) because they would observe his shining dignity and the distinguished qualities of his soul; he

163

whom outsiders would admire: it is him now that everyone here present sees fallen to the earth; him they beweep, him they lament.

And I, indeed the lowliest of the English, commend to you the greatest, and most powerful, a Prince overtaken by death (ah! too soon), so that this honor may be held in his sepulcher, which the dignity of this man, still living to us, merits. And as the distinctions of so outstanding an Englishman enter deeper into your memories and rise into view, his likeness is the more alive before your eyes. I will speak of him, as is fitting, and I will speak truly. But first if I wished to elaborate in vain in praise of our Kingdom, a thing known to you and a familiar from going over it often, I believe I would be pounding your ears more than it is right. On account of this, now that I am omitting the celebration of the Kingdom, I will reflect first upon his lineage to you, so that out of the renown of his stock, you may gather the nobility of this young man.

Among the household history records, we read that the Courtenay family, after the history of their line became illustrious, was famous through portraits and quite outstanding amid the magnificence of Britain. For already from the very start (as far as one may pursue in memory) the Earls of Devon were of this very family. On account of this, since they had many outstanding services towards the republic, they were most often considered deserving for the ties of royal marriage. And from among all the other deserving suitors, Lord William, Earl of Devon, the grandfather of this young man, took the daughter of King Edward IV, Catherine, in marriage, by whom he begat Lord Henry, his [Edward's] father. It was on these grounds that Henry employed the sign of the White rose by maternal right, the emblem of the most illustrious House of York, since the Lancaster's, the leaders of the other faction, always wore the red rose. Through this royal blood tie, however, William was a brother related by blood to King Henry VII, who took to wife the other, elder daughter of King Edward IV, Elizabeth. It would take long to embark upon praises of this man [Edward] and his grandfather. For if I were to review his [William's] virtues and supreme services towards the Kingdom, I believe I would not reach an end, and words would sooner be lacking to ornament so great a Prince than subject matter to garb him: in the same way a task is seen to be taken up not as a pursuit of praise, but as a resolution upon the appropriate method.

Henry was successor to William: son to father, and the father of this man: but what sort of man, good Lord, was he? A man superior to almost every praise, born an Earl, afterward made Marquess of Exeter through his own merit: A man not from a single town, but the whole world; not of society, but the human race; a light and ornament not for a nation alone, but for the whole world. But in the end he enjoyed an adverse fortune, a thing exceedingly lamentable. He was cast down from all honor, and deprived of life.

After his father died — for whom this young man was his only son — Edward, a mere boy, and innocent, twelve years of age, was forced into harsh detention for around fourteen years because of his father's offences. Throughout the whole of this time he strengthened his own nature with such composure of mind and perseverance that he never succumbed or came apart in any way. Already born by nature to letters, he wrapped himself up entirely in his studies. He was a youth of the highest academic ability, such that his labor took the least effort, and yet his diligence was of the sort which was able to entice ability even out of slowness. In such a way neither the narrowness of a place, nor solitude, nor the loss of liberty called him away from his studies. He then began seizing upon philosophy so avidly, in which he was making such great advances, that no one of the ruling class was on a par with him. Neither did he challenge himself in this alone with that praiseworthy enthusiasm of his, but he scrutinized the intimate sciences of nature, he entered the labyrinths of mathematics, he drained the cup of his enthusiasm to the dregs, with the highest enjoyment and a singular pleasure. He burned with such a great desire to paint pictures that he would easily and laudably express the likeness of whatever he wished upon his tablet. He even handled the lyre with a sonorous range, and with a well ordered variety, so that you would describe absolute perfection in it. Neither was he content in its instruction, nor in the collection of decorations, but he also acquired the Spanish, French, and Italian languages. He took pains in all of these things so diligently, and built his intellect in such a fashion, that he would argue and hold conversation with any Foreigner without any interpreter at all, to great acclaim.

But once Our Queen Mary most Serene, by God's greatest beneficence, and by His own law finally succeeded to the throne, she saw such great qualities illuminated in this youth related to her by three degrees of blood-ties. She pitied that servitude of his, and took his solitude to heart. She called him out of custody for the very first time, gave him freedom, restored his honor, and raised him to the highest rank, so that, as they saluted the most pious works of the Queen, the Earl of Devon was saluted by everyone as the most worthy progeny of his forefathers and most illustrious nobleman.

Since therefore the young Edward Courtenay (by the highest grace and clemency of the Queen) had been freed from prison in this way, and escaped free, he showed himself so adept in everything, and advertised so great a specimen of his virtues, that everyone embraced him not only out of the greatest love, but also respect. He was sober without arrogance, an earl without levity, prudent in speech, cautious in reply, modest in argument, neither boasting of himself, nor excluding others. Saying many things with few words, he followed the spirit rather than the letter. Making use of a familiarity with many, he nevertheless was known intimately by few. And although he was on a par with the ruling class in honor, nevertheless he leveled himself with his inferiors by a certain generous nobility of mind, if indeed he understood any marks of virtue or character to be in their discourse. Moreover, he was so disposed in character to doing everything, and with so ardent a will, that out of all those things which are seemly for decorating a distinguished person, or which are suitable for governing him, not one was lacking to him. And since he was just as remarkable in body as he was excellent in mind-the composition of his limbs possessed of a unity and an elegant relationship of parts; outstanding, and with enviable build — he applied his mind to military discipline. He then in a short time sat on a horse so expertly and suitably for a soldier, and whipped his spear against the target so strongly, and would race impressively on horseback; that you could discern in him the excellence of his forefathers.

But perhaps someone would rather assert that I bestow these things to your ears than think them to be true, and believes either that such things were not in him, or at least not such great things, as great as what I myself have made out of my own words-especially since it is hardly credible that so many virtues could be combined in a single person, which individually are found in the smallest number of people. But others with whom he had intimate society would avow and condemn me of lying, if I am carried away in his commendation longer than is fit.

On which account, since he was so excellent among all others that he turned everyone's eyes to himself; and since he was held in such great esteem among even more; it was their opinion that he was not so much granted to the Kingdom as he was deserving of being its King, and married to a Queen. However, he, by that quality which was his modesty, thought nothing great of himself, and continuously declared himself the most unworthy servant of the Queen, always shrinking away from every ambition. But although we afterwards had by divine wisdom the most powerful Philip, son of Emperor Charles V the most invincible as King of the Realm and husband of the Queen, and although there were still those who seditiously and in disorder incited this youth to arms against the King and Queen, he was mindful of his duty, and of his own good faith, and of his lately received kindnesses. He never wished for anyone to seem ungrateful either in conviction or in counsel towards her by whom he was furnished with so many and such great honors, or for anyone to draw her into danger, through whom he himself was liberated from every danger. It is clear from him how divine was the virtue in him, how truly generous his spirit was, he who would never turn away from duty even for the hope of possessing the Kingdom. He was accused of attacking her majesty: but then it is possible to accuse innocent people. He was examined before the King's leading Courtiers: but then he was honorably released. He overcame suspicion in the case of most things: but then his life was impeccable in respect of everything. [Strype, H/M. 1721, pg. 191]

166

CHAPTER 7. THE LANE LETTERS

This chapter will review a collection of rather interesting letters first published in *Lady Jane Grey, an Historical Tale in 2 volumes* printed for William Lane by the Minerva Press in 1791.

The letters are rather controversial because the source of the letters is unknown and, having reviewed all the information presented in this volume about Edward Courtenay, one must question their validity. It would be easy to regard them as fiction, which is why they have been separated from the main body of this work.

But there is a chance that the letters may be based upon obscure information otherwise lost in history and the letters have been included in this biography about Courtenay because some do contain interesting information and for the questions that they may prompt.

The book, *Lady Jane Grey, an Historical Tale in 2 volumes* contains one hundred and ninety-one pages with no mention of the source of the thirty-two letters it contains. Of the thirty-two letters in which Lady Jane Grey is the main character, ten mention Edward Courtenay.

My review of three of the five known copies of the book did not shed light on their source, as all three books are identical. However, there are records of the Minerva Press, which are contained in *The Minerva Press 1790-1820* by Dorothy Blakey, PhD 1939. Blakey reviewed all the known publications that the Minerva Press released and their sources used in those publications, but regarding *Lady Jane Grey an Historical Tale*, Blakey indicated, "no conjecture as to the authorship can be offered."

Quite possibly William Lane had purchased the original manuscript from an anonymous source while he was at the Minerva Press. This may be supported by this quote from *The Star* in the 26 June 1792 issue: "This may well be called the age of Novels, when Lane, at Minerva, Leadenhall-Street, has paid near two-thousand pounds for manuscripts."

Mentioned in some of these letters is a love affair that Courtenay had with a Laurana de M- that began while they were prisoners in the Tower of London and eventually resulted in their marriage some time later. Having reviewed numerous primary and secondary sources while accumulating data for this edition, I did not discover any mention of a love affair or marriage with a Laurana or any other woman for that matter other than the suggestion of his marriage to Mary and the possibilities of a marriage to Elizabeth.

The original author gives just enough information about this Laurana to begin and maintain a search for her identity, but after an exhaustive search of all the noble Italian and Florentine family ancestries of the period, including the most notable family of Medici, no Laurana was found among the names during that period of time. The original author hinted in the letters that the complete last name of this woman was omitted because of the desire to remain secret and to prevent the wrath that Mary could exert if she found out about the marriage to another woman.

Even if they were married and attempted to keep it a secret as the letters suggest, it would have most certainly been discovered by any of those who were watching Courtenay very closely in England and the other countries that he visited for any treasonous activity.

Furthermore, records of the prisoners in the Tower during the reigns of Henry VIII, Edward VI, Lady Jane Grey, and Mary I show no names matching or even close to those described in the letters. The letters suggest that Thomas Cranmer, Archbishop of Canterbury, imprisoned the Lady Laurana and her mother in the Tower during the reign of Henry VIII for their Catholic views.

The first of the letters about Courtenay is from Lady Anne, possibly a cousin of Lady Jane Grey, to Lady Laurana who had by then settled in a convent in Florence. The letter portrays the events after Mary seized the throne from Lady Jane and mentions the Duke of Northumberland's execution on 23 August, as well as Mary's review of the prisoners in the Tower on 3 August. The new queen created Edward Courtenay, Earl of Devon soon after.

LETTER 19

You have, perhaps, by public report, my friend, heard that Lady Jane is deposed, and Mary acknowledged Queen of England.

Your friendly heart will feel for our distress, and the ill-success of that excellent Lady, who yet would return to private life, with the highest satisfaction, might she hope that Mary's fears would permit her consideration of her as no consequence. She has, indeed, professed to pardon both Lady Jane and her Lord, as well as the Duke of Suffolk; but I distress much that it will be revoked again, as they are not permitted to quit the Tower.

The Duke of Northumberland has suffered for his ambition, and with him two others, who were principals in the party, but no others nearly related to us.

The Queen's lenity has gained her great popularity, in punishing no more on this occasion.

Lord Guildford, who was possessed of the highest filial affection, morns incessantly for his father's violent death, and his affectionate wife shares his grief – they are actuated but by one soul – and it is impossible for either to feel a sorrow, which the other partakes not of.

As soon as Mary arrived at the gates of the Tower, the Duke of Suffolk immediately opened them to her, and was the first to acknowledge her his rightful Sovereign. Mortifying, indeed, was this to him, who was compelled to it by necessity, as he knew of Northumberland's defeat.

But when Lady Jane received the haughty Mary, and laid her crown at her feet, with the sweet humility, equally free from meanness or fear, Mary seemed struck with the greatness of her manner; her eyes were disarmed, for a moment, of that fierce anger, which flashed from them at her entrance; and filled with a sentiment of admiration, mixed with envy, that vice of little minds, which cannot yield an entire and unpolluted tribute of praise to virtue, she affected to treat her as a poor deluded child, the object only of her contempt, and beneath her anger.

On Mary's entrance into the Tower, she also enquired what prisoners of state were there, and demanded to see them; they presented themselves to her, and she pardoned them all; among the rest the Duke of Norfolk and Courtney.

Mary was exceedingly struck with the person of the latter, and though unacquainted with the manners and ceremonies of the court, the ease and dignity that are natural to him, she thought far preferable to the artful address of the courtier.

She immediately reinstated Norfolk and him into their honors and estates, and created Courtney, Earl of Devon. – No nobleman about the court is at present in such high favor with the Queen, and all the ladies of it; he has began to apply himself to learn those accomplishments, and active exercises, which his long captivity has withheld from him the means of acquiring.

It is imagined, by some people, that the Queen is strongly attached to him; and, as his rank is noble, and he is an Englishman, it is thought, she will contrive that an alliance with him shall be proposed to the people.

And now, my fair friend, you tremble for your lover; yet comfort yourself, and do not despair; I am certain he will never marry the Queen. He has privately visited us several times; he has informed us of every thing doing at court, and declares that he could not, without the greatest aversion, consider Mary in the light of a wife, was he not engaged to you by every tie of honor and affection.

He speaks highly of the Princess as a friend, who possesses eminent virtues and merit, but says, he shall never cease to love his Laurana, in preference to all the women he ever saw; though he acknowledges, that he fears the Queen will never permit him to marry you. He entreats me to renew to you his vows of eternal constancy. He says, he shall rejoice if the

Queen will appoint him any foreign service, which may enable him to see you again, but he fears she will not suffer him to quit the Kingdom.

He would request your return to England, but that he should be fearful of your safety, if the Queen, by any means, discovered your connection: this has hitherto prevented his writing to you; but he says, he will now write to you himself, and enclose his letter in mine. You may now, therefore, correspond through this medium; for to own the truth, Mary does really love the Earl, and her temper is suspicious to a great degree.

I am rejoiced to find, by the return of your conductor, that your voyage was agreeable, and that you are settled in a convent at Florence, which you knew something of. – I am impatient for a more particular account of your health, and enjoyment of some share of tranquility.

Adieu,

Anne Grey [Lane, Vol. II 10].

In her reply to Lady Anne, Laurana speaks of the danger of remaining in England, collateral corroboration of her secret affection for Edward Courtenay.

LETTER 20

I promised you, my dear Lady Anne, in the short letter which I writ you, by the person sent to conduct me to this convent, a longer one very soon, though I have not yet received one from you.

I will proceed to inform you of a circumstance, which is a very pleasing one to me; it is, that I have found a cousin in the convent I am in. – Heaven surely directed me here for consolation! – My parents lost to me by death, torn by a cruel necessity from that lover, and those dear, and newly acquired friends, I possessed in the Queen and yourself, my fate seemed peculiarly cruel during my voyage.

Your excellent Lady Jane had restored to me the patrimony of my parents, so that I obtained a friendly reception from the abbess, from whom I concealed my real name; but for some time, my heart was ready to break, from the consideration of the happiness I had lost, and the lonely, and comfortless situation I was in. – My mind too enlightened, to relish the dull and superstitious routine of a convent life; the cold and formal prayers, so frequently offered by the lips, whilst the heart is absent and unaffected; disgusted by the malevolent passions, and petty competitions, and all the uninteresting events of the nunnery, as well as the mean and artful methods which they took, to induce me to assume the veil.

I most earnestly wished, at times, that I had taken a lodging in England; but perfectly convinced how dangerous, and disagreeable, my unprotected state would have been, utterly ignorant as I am of the world, I was restrained by this consideration from returning.

My mind was in this disgusted situation, when one day, a nun, who had always been inclined to show me every proof of friendship, and whose pleasing person and manner attracted my regard, observing a picture on my bracelet, which was that of my father, suddenly became pale as death, trembled, and was ready to faint: I had remarked her attention to the picture, and much alarmed at the emotion it was the occasion of, flew to assist her, and when a little returned to herself, at my earnest request, she told me that the picture I wore, was that of an uncle extremely dear to her, but whose severity had caused her great and heavy afflictions.

"You are then my cousin," said I, transported with delight, "how happy am I to find so near a relation in a person, for whom I felt a peculiar partiality; I shall now find my situation less painful to me! – How long is it since I have known the sweet pleasure of family connections! Refuse me not your love, my dear cousin, though my father *did* treat you severely; and repose so much confidence in me, as to make me acquainted with my family affairs and connections, to which I am entire stranger."

"Is it possible, my dear, that you are not acquainted with the reason of your father's quitting Florence! – But you shall hear my sad and affecting story – at present, however, you must excuse it; my spirits are overcome with the surprise, pain, and joy which I received at the sight of the picture, and the certainly that the wearer of it is my cousin.

"Yes, my dear Laurana, you do posses my sincerest affection; my heart was also attracted to you from the first moment you entered the convent; greatly was I charmed with your person and manners, and affected at your dejection of spirits. – I often tried to account to myself, for my irresistible prepossession in your favor, but could not do it; but I now discern it to be the effect of natural sympathy, that your happiness interested me, as much as if you had been a sister, though you were so lately a stranger to me. – May a firm and lasting friendship unite us, and render this abode of melancholy gloom more pleasing to us both."

My cousin, who goes by the name of sister Clara, is about twenty-eight; her person a feminine likeness of my father, but a much greater sweetness diffused over her countenance; her complexion is clear, but pale; and her eyes languidly beautiful; her whole form elegant and interesting, though wrap up in the dress of a nun. She has worn the veil nearly ten years, and is universally beloved by all the deserving part of the convent.

The next day, she came into my room, and told me, that she would relate to me the events of her life, which, with many interruptions from her feelings, she did as follows:

"Your father, my dear Laurana, was the only surviving one of many brothers which mine had, and, at his decease, which I was too young to remember any thing of, he put my fortune and myself into his guardianship, who had not then been long married. I was treated by both your father and mother, with great tenderness; had every proper advantage of education and grew up exceedingly happy under their protection.

When I was about seventeen, I was one evening walking with my governess by the water-side, and was accosted by some fellows in a boat, that was rowing by me, in a very licentious manner, though they wore the dress of gentlemen. I was immediately retiring, when one of them jumped out and was attempting to seize me and place me in the boat; when a gentleman, who had been sitting on a bench, with a book in his hand, suddenly flew to my assistance, and rescued me in a moment from the ruffian, by striking him down with a stick which he held, and, before any of the others had power to go to his assistance, carried me off.

A service so signal, gave the young man a genteel reception with my uncle an aunt, and made no small impression on my young heart, which had never before felt the tender passion.

He was received as a welcome guest whenever he visited us, and soon found means of informing and persuading me of his violent attachment, and obtained the return he wished for; yet it was a long time, however, before he would speak himself to my uncle, or allow me to mention our mutual affection to my aunt.

He said, as his family was of much higher rank than ours, he was certain his father would never consent to the alliance, nor in that case, could I suppose, my friends would permit him to visit me; that, therefore, if I did not think to be separated for ever from him, we must be silent, and conceal our connection.

After some time, I was sought in marriage by a considerable nobleman, whom I refused; at which my uncle was exceedingly enraged, and insisted on my recalling my refusal, and marrying him. He was, indeed, in point of person, fortune, and character, unexceptionable, had I not unhappily been pre-engaged; but this also I refused to do: for though I always considered my uncle as another father, I did not think his authority extended so far, as to control my inclination, in an affair where the happiness of my life was concerned.

Fired to an extreme degree at this opposition to his will, he accused me of carrying on an intrigue with the Count de R-.

I was so much irritated at this accusation, that, I believe, I said some provoking things on the subject. I was conscious of his honor, and my own virtue, and could not support the idea of being suspected of the contrary, and, perhaps, said more than I ought.

My uncle went immediately to the Count's father, and acquainted him with what he suspected of our mutual attachment; not that I think he believed, nor certainly would he have insinuated to him, that our connection was a dishonorable one; but that there was any connection, was enough for the enraged father of the Count; whose pride was extreme, and who had the most ambitious views for his son.

He immediately sent for him into his presence; accused him of this affair, and told him, that unless he would consent to give it instantly up, by the same hour the next evening, he would insist on his taking the habit, and would make his brother his sole heir.

The Count was thunder-struck at this communication, though it was what he had every reason to expect from his father, should he be informed of his attachment.

He remonstrated all in his power, and respectfully entreated his haughty father to see the object of his affection, but all in vain; neither the rank nor fortune was equal; and those were the only things worthy of estimation in his eyes.

He could not see me that evening, and, therefore, wrote to entreat my consent to the only thing that could possibly soften his father in my favor, who, he was persuaded, when he knew it was irretrievable, would become reconciled to the alliance: a private marriage was what he proposed, but he forbore to say what his father had threatened him with.

His eloquence was all-prevailing with me, though I have, a thousand times since, condemned my conduct. I met him early the next morning, and sat off with him to some distance from Florence, where we could be privately married.

By some means, or other, our route was traced, and the enraged father of my lover pursued us, accompanied by my uncle, and the ceremony was just finished, when they entered the church in which we were.

Claps of thunder, and the elements in the utmost fury, could not have appalled us so much as this intrusion. My lover knew his doom. – His father forced him from me; but I became insensible, by violent faintings, and could not be removed for many hours; fits succeeding each other with violence, threatened to tear the agonized soul from its feeble tenement.

At length, I was conducted home, and threatened to be put into a convent, if I did not conceal this contract of marriage, which they both pretended to believe was not concluded when they arrived, and consent the next day to listen to the gentleman whom my uncle had designed for me.

My soul turned with horror from this proposal, and I refused to quit my apartment, where I spent a week in an agony, which language, the most expressive would fail in describing.

At the end of that time I received a letter from my husband, saying, that, after a deal of threatening and persuasion, his father had disinherited him, and turned him from his house; but that he had a small estate, which he could not rob him of, being a legacy left him by a friend. That this little annuity, with me, would be riches to him, if I would condescend to fly with him to Geneva, or some cheap place, where we might live on it, with frugality, in felicity.

That he had empowered his friend, in whose hands it was, to remit to us the income of it quarterly; that for his part, he should regret nothing but my being reduced to poverty, and denied those elegancies which I had been accustomed to.

Transported with joy at this letter, I instantly packed up what clothes I could, and all my jewels, and sent them, in small parcels, by my woman, who had been my confident, and was resolved to share my destiny, by attending me in my flight.

We left the house in the evening; my husband met us, and we traveled incessantly till we thought ourselves out of danger of a second pursuit, before we ventured to take any rest or refreshment.

We arrived safely at Geneva, found out a beautiful little cottage, near the lake, where we settled, and found that sincere happiness, which can only be enjoyed in the married state, where love and friendship intermingle their garlands. The only alloy to it, which I felt, was the consideration that my husband had forfeited his father's blessing and inheritance, which obliged him to worse accommodations than his high birth had accustomed him to.

After some time had expired, however, I observed that my husband became thoughtful and melancholy. He was frequently subject to an absence of thought in conversation, and no longer enjoyed his usual amusements.

My heart, fond of him to destruction, took the alarm, nor would I permit him to rest, till I had obtained the cause of his uneasiness, which arose from his having offended his father, and forfeited his favor and blessing.

He said, he did not regard his being cut off from his inheritance, but he could not support the idea of his father dying, and leaving his with his curse on his head; and he longed to go and throw himself at his feet, and, if possible, get this imprecation recalled, or otherwise could enjoy no peace, though otherwise as blest as man could be.

I did not oppose his journey, and he left me. O fatal hour when I permitted him to do it! but to see him miserable! – him for whom I would have gladly sacrificed my own existence! – it was not in nature. A most mournful farewell did we take of each other.

I wanted to accompany him, but he would not suffer it, and he went attended only by his faithful valet.

An age of time I thought had passed before I heard any intelligence of or from him, and when I did hear from him, it was the happy tidings, that his father was reconciled to him, and approved of his choice; and that the bearer of this letter was to convey me to Florence.

You may imagine that my joy was without bounds. But I must pursue my husband's footsteps for a while, and pass over my own feelings.

His journey was a gloomy one, full of apprehensions, though without shrinking for a moment from his purpose.

He arrived at his father's house, and demanded to see him. – He was introduced to a man whose vindictive rage, and offended pride, were painted in every feature of his face.

He accosted him in the humblest manner on his knees, and implored him to pardon a son, who had never before willfully offended him; who was impelled, by a fatal attachment, to disobey him, but could enjoy no happiness while under a father's interdiction.

Unsoftened by all his prayers and remonstrance's, his features relinquished nothing of their angry expression, but rather became more inflamed.

He told him, he had no other alternative for him now, but to take religious orders; and he would be confined in the house that night, and the next day sent to the convent. That if he complied with this his fixed determination, discovered suitable penitence, perhaps he might one day forgive him.

He was taken forcibly from his father's presence, like a convict, and conducted to his apartment, where, the next day, a monk was sent to him, and endeavored to persuade him to make his peace with his father, and consent to enter into religious orders.

But all his endeavors to that effect being vain, the artful priest took another method to prevail on him:

He went to him a few hours after, with great appearance of joy and friendship in his countenance, and told him, his father would consent to see his wife; and if he approved of her conversation and behavior, he would be reconciled to him and the alliance.

My husband, rejoiced almost to distraction, and totally off his guard, said, he would set out immediately for Geneva and fetch her.

"And is she really so far off as Geneva? said the monk. The count satisfied him with the greatest minuteness where she was, and the monk told him, that he would hasten and inform his father where his wife resided, who would, he doubted not, send for her immediately. The Count was eagerly urging his own departure for that purpose, but the monk was out of the room in an instant.

He immediately went and communicated to the Count's father, the artifice he had used, to obtain the knowledge of my abode. "And now, Seignior," said he, "you may either send for her and confine her, and thus separate them for ever; or, you may threaten him with whatever you please, to obtain of your son, his consent to become a monk.

The father was delighted with this scheme, and thought, at all events, he ought to secure me in his power, and therefore sent for me; ordering his son to write to me, and to advise me to enter into a convent for a little while, till my uncle also could be talked to, and persuaded to be reconciled to me.

Thus, you see my husband himself assisted to throw me into their snares; but, incapable himself of such villainy, he little suspected his father could be guilty of it.

As to myself, my husband's handwriting left me without any doubt on my mind. I settled my little affairs, and sat out with the highest satisfaction; yet, I left my neat little cottage with regret, where I had enjoyed so much real felicity. I was safely conducted to the convent; where I hourly waited, with the utmost impatience, to see again my husband.

The Duke, satisfied that he had me in safety, never thought of seeing me, or concerning himself any more about me, only to order the superior, not to admit any visitors to me, but what came from himself.

The Duke, and his vile agent, then pursued their scheme, acquainting the poor deluded son, that all he had said, was to get his pretended wife into his power; and that now he expected that he would obey him, and determine on a conventual life, for that he never again would see his mistress; and if he did not consent, her situation would be far from agreeable.

Irritated by violent contending passions; filled with all the rage that could animate a human breast, at this injurious treatment; and feeling the utmost contempt for that state of life, which produced such a villain as the monk, he gave vent to all the indignation it inspired him with, in the most furious and unrestrained language; then, snatching up his sword, which he saw at the farther end of the room, on a chair, he plunged it through his body, with that haste and violence, that he fell down before his persecutors had time to fly and prevent him.

The monk hastily quitted the apartment: the haughty Duke, as if struck through the heart with remorse, stood immovably fixed to the place, till my husband, in a faint voice, earnestly requested that he might be permitted to see his wife before he died.

Roused by this request, he bid his servant, who was in the room, to go and conduct me to him, and also to order a surgeon immediately, who soon came, but found it was too late to do any thing for his recovery, the wound being undoubtedly mortal.

Overwhelmed with horror and distress, I received this dreadful intelligence, at the very moment when I expected to see my dear husband enter, full of transport and felicity: but the sight of the man, dear to me as my life, weltering in his blood; struck by his own rash hand, and about to quit me for ever, was a sight too dreadful to support, and the recollection affects me too much to enlarge on it.

He died the next day, penitent, and full of remorse for his precipitation.

The unhappy father bitterly repented of his cruelty. He sent for my uncle, and offered to settle whatever he thought proper on me, and to consider me as his daughter.

But I resolutely refused his offered bounty, and persisted in taking the veil, and ending my days, which I hoped would not be long, in this convent.

My uncle deeply felt this melancholy scene, and regretted, with extreme sorrow and self-condemnation, the part he had it its promotion, by obliging me to quit his house, to avoid a hatred alliance.

He entreated me to return to his house with him, and promised, I believe with great sincerity, that he would contribute every thing in his power to restore my spirits, and render me happy.

I told him, there was no happiness for me on earth, and a life of religious retirement was the only state which suited, and would, in any respect, sooth my grief.

I soon after returned to my convent, and, at the end of my novicate, took the veil, in the presence of my relations.

My uncle regretting so much, even to the last, my resolution, that he was disgusted with Florence, and went to reside in England; to which he was still farther induced, by the horrid situation of my husband's father, whose distraction of mind was of the most dreadful nature, uttering vengeance from Heaven on himself and the monk, whom he never after would suffer in his fight.

My husband was his favorite son, and he had always treated him with great affection; but his pride of birth, his son's opposition to his will, and to the schemes he had been for many years planning to aggrandize him, all crushed at once, by his marriage with me, so overcame parental tenderness, and wounded his haughty spirit, that he felt no concern for his happiness, and sought nothing but to hide him in the obscurity of a convent, that he might transfer all his lofty schemes to his brother.

But the fatal end of his unhappy son dissipated his ambitious views, mortified his pride, and awoke his soul to all a father's tenderness; and the remorse consequent to his cruelty to a son so amiable, shook his reason, and destroyed his intellects, for he never again recovered them, but death, a few years after, dissolved his worn-out frame, and his freed soul entered into the presence of his Maker.

It was a long time before I recovered my tranquility, or could raise wishes and views beyond this frail mortality, though I had nothing to attract me to it, nothing to engage my affections. The past, not the future, possessed my thoughts, tied me down to vain regret and discontent; and, alas, how far is this from that disposition which constitutes a real devotee.

I have, however, for some years past, been tolerably composed; but shall I own, My Laurana, that the fight of you, and the picture of my uncle, has brought to my too lively recollection the past events of my life, and renewed my sad regrets. Nor has this relation of them to you tended, in a small degree, to this end.

Ah! would Heaven be pleased to conclude my tiresome warfare, and place me above the reach of restless discontent and useless regrets.

You have the world before you – you are again to put out to sea, and struggle with the billows of life. Ought I not rejoice, that I am in a secure haven, and have only the acquisition of patience and resignation to attain for a little, a very little time, when I shall only have the narrow gulph of death to cross, and then be happy for ever.

My cousin finished her story with tears, which had frequently interrupted her in her narration, and mine slowed plentifully in sympathy with her. You will not, I am certain, refuse her your compassion and esteem.

I must now close this long letter; may I soon receive yours. I am anxious to hear what is become of the Earl of Devon, as I have not yet heard from him. Adieu. May all happiness attend my dear Lady Anne and her friends.

Laurana de M-

P.S. I have received your, and the Earl's letters – am shocked and grieved at their contents. The disposition of Lady Jane, the death of the Duke of Northumberland, and the danger of all your friends concerned in her party. – O, what shall I say to console you? Let us hope that Heaven will not permit such virtue as Lady Jane's to suffer; and yet is virtue an exemption from suffering on earth? – Alas, no. How many fatal proofs have I had of that? I cannot deny that I tremble also for my Courtney. Impatiently shall I wait for your letters. Do not fail to write me by every possible conveyance.

Farewell [Lane, Vol. II 19].

Lady Anne's letter to Lady Laurana mentions the need to keep their correspondence a secret from Mary. Had Mary intercepted any of the letters, their fate could have been grim. It was well known that for a short period of time, Courtenay was considered as a worthy husband for Mary as the following letter mentions.

LETTER 21

I am exceedingly glad, my dear friend, that you have mine and the Earl's letters, both, as the proofs of his constancy have given relief to the anxieties of your mind, in some degree, and because we were very fearful that they had been intercepted by the Queen, whose jealously causes her to set spies on all his actions.

Her hatred to the Lady Elizabeth increases daily, and the friends of that Princess are apprehensive that her life is in danger. She has caused overtures of marriage to be made to Devonshire, who has rejected them in a manner, as little offensive to the Queen's pride and love as possible; yet she is highly enraged with him, though her pride will not suffer her to discover her disappointment publicly; and, I think, the Earl had best quit the Kingdom as soon as possible.

He has recovered his health, but a look of dejection hangs over his blooming countenance, which he takes evident pains to conceal. He is become particularly expert in all the manly exercises of youth, and experiences a still greater degree of pleasure in them, from his having been so many years deprived of them. Yet those years of confinement was not loss time to him, but were diligently applied to the cultivation of his mind, of his patience, fortitude, habits of reflection, and philosophy, and convinced him of the vanity of greatness and ambition; though of a faith contrary to my own, I have the charity to believe him beloved by heaven; and as for him, he has too much liberality of mind to be a bigot, and despises sincerely Mary's ignorance and blind zeal.

I think, that to abjure a religion, let it be what it will, in which your conscience still acquiesces, is a meanness that I should scorn myself, or any of my friends for doing; but, if those friends thought me in error, and persuaded me to hear arguments on the other side, I would not shut my ears to conviction, but use every method, by the reason which God hath given me, to discern the truth.

I would not have the Scriptures of truth concealed from me in a language I did not understand, but with them in my hand, I would pray for enlightened grace to understand them aright. Thus, it is my opinion, we shall either be preserved from error, or (provided our lives are virtuous) our errors will be harmless.

But not so the Queen; she has refused to hear any arguments in favor of the reformation; she has abolished the laws of Edward, and restored the Romish religion, which last, as a Catholic, you will be pleased at; but when I tell you that she has began a cruel persecution, and that many bishops, and even many of our sex, have sealed their testimony to the belief of the Protestant faith with their blood! Will not your gentle nature revolt at the horrid idea? Will prejudices, imbibed in infancy, so totally warp the natural sensibility of your temper, as to occasion no feelings of detestation for a persecuting spirit and pity for the noble sufferers?

Ah! my friend, you have undergone an irksome captivity for your own faith, and from Protestants too. How injurious to any cause, persecution wherever found. How contrary to the genius of true religion. – Can that be truth, which fear exacts from the professing lip? Can persecution work conviction in the heart? Or frail men imagine they can perform the work of God?

I am very glad you have found a near relation, and amiable friend, in your solitude, my dear Laurana. Her story is, indeed, a melancholy one: – may she find every consolation that is in the power of religion to give her.

Lord Guildford is more reconciled to his father's fate; and all my dear friends begin so far to recover their usual tranquility, as to reassume their usual employments and studies; as the Queen has released them, and permitted them to return to their habitation in town: but the instability of the times, and the gloomy prospects which we have before us, have led us rather to fix on those studies, which will invigorate our minds with fortitude and true philosophy, to encounter whatever trials may be appointed us.

From the life and sufferings of the divine founder of our faith, and his faithful martyrs, and the noble lessons imparted to us by them, in that treasury of divine knowledge withheld from you by mercenary priests; by these we have the most effectual instructions in fortitude: greatly do I fear, that we shall need all the aids they can give us. – Alas! Mary, whose resentments are implacable, has not spared my young friends, I fear, but from political reasons.

Forgive me, my friend, the melancholy letters I write you: how pleasing and delightful would be the present scene before me, might I hope their happiness would continue.

Beloved and affectionate parents, in the Duke and Duchess of Suffolk. A married pair, inspired with all the tender assiduity and ardor of lovers, in Lord Guildford and Lady Jane: while your friends loses almost the thoughts of her own concerns, in contemplating their felicity and dreading a reverse. They have, however, an allay to their comfort, in the illness of Lady Catherine, who is still at S – , as her weakness will not permit her to travel.

I have not yet quitted them, but my father wishes for some share of my company, and I cannot be so lost to the duty and affection I owe him, as not to attend him.

I am, with sincere regard, dear Lady Laurana,

Your Anne Grey [Lane, Vol. II 63].

Lady Anne wrote Lady Laurana, describing the beginning of the conflicts regarding the announcement of Mary's choice for a

husband in the first part of the letter. In the second part she gave
more details after a short amount of time had passed.

> Again is this unhappy kingdom torn to pieces by a civil war. – The
> Queen is about to form a Spanish alliance: the people are incensed at it, as
> Don Philip is a foreigner and a Catholic, and have been induced to take up
> arms: in many different counties are they shedding each other's blood
> with utmost violence. – How prophetic my fears, that we should not long
> enjoy the peaceful domestic pleasures which I described to you in my last
> letter.
>
> The Duke of Suffolk has quitted us for some days past: we have a
> thousand apprehensions, lest he should be persuaded to join the insur-
> gents. The Duchess has sent messengers every where, but cannot hear any
> tidings of him, where he usually resorted.
>
> Both Lady Jane, and her Lord, most sincerely wish their father to for-
> bear all pursuits of ambition, by which his family have suffered so much:
> he is not formed for them: in domestic life he is truly amiable; there he
> shines in every character; but he has never yet done so in a public one. We
> all, with the greatest impatience, wait the return of the messengers.
>
> Since I wrote the above, the Earl of Devon has been here, and has con-
> firmed our fears; informing us, that the Duke has indeed been prevailed on
> to join the male-contents. As soon as he heard of it, he flew to acquaint us
> with it, and prepare us for what might be the event. I cannot describe to
> you the grief of this family, and our suspense is almost intolerable.
>
> Lord Guildford is very desirous of joining his father-in-law, but we
> all, with the greatest earnestness, entreat he will not. My father and uncle
> are with him, I find, which distracts me a thousand fears for their safety.
>
> I will not conclude this letter, till I have further information; God
> grant it may be fortunate. Adieu.

Continuation:

> Ah, my friend! new scenes of horror are preparing for us. My silence
> has been a long one, and the vicissitudes numerous, which have filled up
> the time since I began this letter. The consequent alarm, and anxious sus-
> pense in which it has kept my mind, would not permit me to finish it.
>
> The Duke of Norfolk is taken, in endeavoring to raise the people of
> Warwick and Leicester, where his interest lay. He was pursued at the
> head of three hundred horse, obliged to disperse his followers, and fly to

conceal himself; but his concealment was soon discovered, and he was carried prisoner to London.

As the Duke was encouraged to join the rebels by their promises to restore Lady Jane, if they succeeded, to the throne, you may imagine that the Queen's resentment is highly irritated against him and his family. The other male-contents are also subdued; and Sir Thomas Wyatt, the principle instigator of the rebellion, is condemned and executed. Four hundred persons are said to have suffered in this insurrection, and as many more were pardoned by the Queen, to whom they were conducted with ropes about their necks.

I have no hope remaining, that either the Duke of Suffolk, or his children, will be spared; and this afflicted, though innocent family, are now waiting, with painful suspense, the fate of their husband and father, and their own. - I also dread lest my father should share the same unhappy fate. I flew to enquire for him, but found he was not yet taken. - O, that he may escape!

And now, my dear Lady Laurana, prepare your heart; you have need also of fortitude, if you love the Earl of Devon: the vindictive Queen has again sent him into confinement, though perfectly innocent of the crime with which he is charged.

On the examination of Wyatt, he had accused the Lady Elizabeth, and the Earl of Devon, as accomplices; but on the scaffold, acquitted them, before the people, of having any share in his rebellion. However, on his first accusation of them, Mary immediately had her sister arrested, under a strong guard, and sent to the Tower; here, however, she did not stay long; the dying declaration of Wyatt, obliged the Queen to release her: but she soon after found a pretence to imprison her again, and sent her to Woodstock; and also confined the Earl, though equally innocent, in Fotheringay Castle. - What havoc does human passion cause in the world, unguided by wisdom and virtue!

I will write to you again, if I am able to do so, when the cup of fate is filled. - I cannot afford you any consolation at present, my friend; horrible images of death present themselves continually before my eyes.

How earnestly do I pray for the fortitude of Lady Jane. - How do I admire her noble steady mind, rising with a divine radiance, above the thick cloud of fate which hovers around her. - When will it break! When will the thunder burst from it, which thus oppresses us with its intolerable weight! - O God! prepare us for the event!

Anne Grey [Lane, Vol. II 74].

The following letter from Lady Anne to Catherine sister of Lady Jane Grey gives the most information about Laurana.

Unfortunately, not enough information is given to substantiate her existence. Lady Anne also describes in great detail the love affair between Laurana and Courtenay that began as prisoners in the Tower.

LETTER 27

Your sister, my Catherine, acquits herself, in her exalted situation, with the same humility and affability as in private life. There is in her noble air, a seriousness which seems to arise from the apprehension of insecurity in her new dignity, and a painful idea of not holding it by a lawful claim. This indeed, she has frequently expressed, but her father and friends endeavor to reassure her.

As soon as she was at liberty from the multitude of cares and business, which she was at once involved in, she enquired what prisoners were in the Tower, and ordered them to be brought to her in turn, that she might attend to their claims. Many amongst them she heard, and set at liberty.

The Duke of Norfolk, and Courtney, son of the Marquis of Exeter, were at last introduced to her. Her tender and compassionate heart was melted at the sight of the venerable Norfolk, attained, as he had been, by Harry the VIIIth on no crime, but his superior family honors and greatness, and being one of the first Noblemen in the Kingdom.

How many years had he been immured here, lost to the world and his country; as had also the young and amiable Courtney, who possess a most elegant person and gentle manners, but, being confined so young, appeared ignorant of many accomplishments necessary to a young nobleman; an air of dejection, mixed with resignation, sat on his pale countenance, the sensibility and dignity of which prepossessed all hearts in his favor. He was, also, committed without any crime of his own, when his father was attained.

An amiable and pleasing Lady was next presented, by the desire of Courtney, who professed himself deeply interested in her welfare. When she was introduced to the Queen, and, after her first address to her, on looking round the room, she suddenly became faint, and was falling down, when I perceived her emotion, which, I thought, proceeded from her discovering Courtney among the company; but every one else, I believe, imputed it to the effects of sickness, which her countenance evidently wore the traces of.

She soon, however, recovered her spirits, and said, she was imprisoned by Bishop Cranmer's Councils to the Protector, in the beginning of Edward's reign, and also a mother, who was since dead; that her crime was an adherence to her religion, which was the Catholic.

The noble freedom with which she acknowledged this, pleased Lady Jane, as it did me, and we entreated the Duke of Suffolk to permit her to remain with us, which he willingly consented to; at the same time saying, that the Lady was at liberty, whenever she chose, to quit the Tower. But the Duke of Norfolk and Courtney were not permitted to enjoy that liberty, till the new Queen was a little more established, though they had leave to walk where they pleased within the Tower walls.

As soon as we were alone with the lovely Lady Laurana de M-, I entreated her to inform us of the principle incidents of her life, if it was not disagreeable to her; that the young nobleman, who had last been examined, professed himself interested warmly in her happiness, and that I had observed they both seemed much affected at their meeting in the Queen's presence, though respect for her had kept them silent, or some other motive to me unknown.

Tears of sensibility filled her eyes at my request, and flowed down her pale cheek, on which dejection had deeply preyed.

After a little pause, she said, she was much obliged to me for the concern I took in her affairs, and would most willingly comply with my request, which she immediately did.

LADY LAURANA'S STORY

My family is Italian, and noble, of the house of M-. My parents had some years been settled in England, having quitted their own city, Florence, on account of a tragical family event, which had given them a disgust to it, and wounded their hearts too deeply to permit them again to reside in it.

I was their only child, and brought up in their faith. At length my father died, and my mother still continued here, living as the gentry of this kingdom, but not in a splendid or conspicuous manner, for the greatly preferred retirement.

In the beginning of Edward's reign, the Kingdom was divided with religious disputes, which were carried on with such violence and inveteracy, that the spirit of persecution was very prevalent even among Protestants, though they greatly condemned the Catholics for it; and the Protector was too much guided by Bishop Cranmer, in imprisoning, and frequently punishing with torture, those who differed from them, in matters which were deemed by each party essential; so that even women did not escape their tyranny. Amongst the rest my mother and myself, young as I then was, not more than twelve years old, were imprisoned for our obstinacy in our principles.

Thus you see, Madam, that my heart has early learnt to suffer. While my mother lived, however, it was tolerable to me; her conversation and instructions, in every part of education, which she was completely accomplished in, filled up great part of our time. We had a guitar, with some music and other books, which we studied till we had them by heart; and being permitted sometimes to take a little air, the confinement seemed to me so much like that of a nunnery, that it did not cost me my cheerfulness; and my mother endeavoured to maintain her's, that she might render my lot more tolerable. – But, alas! at the end of four years, my dear mother died, after a lingering illness, occasioned, doubtless, by her misfortunes, and the regrets she felt on my account, which, as she carefully kept them from, injured her health still more effectually.

I had watched over her with unremitting attention, during her tedious decay; but, when I found she was gone for ever, my grief was so violent and excessive, that they could scarcely tear me away from the insensible body, which I fondly hung over, and suffered more than it is in the power of language to describe in the contemplation of. They conveyed me into another apartment, in a very different part of the Tower.

For a while I gave myself up to sorrow, nor could any thing divert my attention from it; but I sat stupid and unemployed by any of my former avocations. For some months I continued in this way; looking out at my little grated window was the only amusement I took.

The anxieties of my mind were, at length, by slow degrees, relived, by the voice of a young man confined in the next apartment to mine. At first I paid little attention to him; and if I did, it was with a disgust, as music but ill-accorded with my grief. But, by degrees, as it abated, I began to listen to him, by way of amusement.

It was a long time before I had the pleasure of seeing him; but the sound of his voice was familiar to me, both in singing and reading, which he always did aloud, frequently poetry, which he recited with a great deal of taste and judgment.

I had formed a pleasing idea of him, from the knowledge I had of his sentiments: he would frequently, in his poetry, lament, in the most pathetic manner, the loss of liberty; being shut up from the charms of society, the difficulty which he had to obtain knowledge and improvement of mind, and the desire of those endearing family connections which blest his childhood; then would he solace his mind with the reflection, that the tyranny of others, and not his own guilt, had occasioned this long confinement, which gave him still a hope that Providence would, some way or other, procure the means of his deliverance.

He too well painted his own lot, not to penetrate my heart with a lively sense of his grief, as well as his merit; and, indeed, these amusements were the only ones which I enjoyed.

I received great improvement from the books he read, which were frequently on learned and studious subjects; sometimes religious; from these last, I found he was of the Romish church.

It was near three months, that this invisible youth entertained me daily, unconscious of the pleasure he gave. One day, looking out at my window, I saw a young man walking in a little garden, into which it looked; the dignity of his air, and the elegance of his person, though in disabille, excited my attention. I had frequently seen people walking there, but none had ever gained from me a moment's notice. I secretly wished this might be the unknown person, who had so greatly gained upon my esteem and sympathy.

As he walked, he cast his eyes up at the windows, and at last fixed them on mine. – I attracted his observation; he looked more eagerly at my face, and at last obliged me to retire, from a sentiment of modesty, which would not permit me to support so steady an observer. I, several days after this, saw the young man, who always paid me the same attention; but the garden was too closely guarded to permit him to speak, had he wished it.

One evening, as the refulgent radiance, with which the moon shone through my little grated casement, invited me to open it, while the recollection of those rural pleasures I has been accustomed to enjoy before my captivity; the charming scenes of variegated nature, which I remembered with peculiar delight, mixed with melancholy at the thoughts of enjoying them no longer, at last, imperceptibly introduced my dear departed mother to my mind, with many tender scenes of my childhood and youth, when I was the object of all her cares.– I know not how long I was engaged in these reveries, but that I was recalled from them by the well-known voice in the garden, who sung to his guitar the following words:

I.
How sweet the rose – the lilly fair,
The morn of spring serene;
How sweet the summer's closing day,
And moonlight's silver scene.
II.
But sweeter far the gen'rous heart,
With friendship's flame imprest;
Or the first dawn of tender love,
Which fires the artless breast.
III.

But where are nature's pleasing powers,
While darkness spreads its gloom?
And distant from the fragrant flowers,
We lose the sweet perfume.

IV.

Thus when the night of absence reigns,
The joys of converse shed;
Fair friendship droops, and plaintive strains,
Declare all pleasure dead.

I looked out with caution, lest he should observe my curiosity; but finding his eyes fixed on the window, I hastily withdrew myself; he then sung and played another air, expressive of love, and regret for the loss of liberty.

I shut the window hastily, and retired to my bed; but it was only to ruminate over this incident, in which I felt an excess of pain and pleasure. - Greatly rejoiced was I to be assured that this young man was the same person, whose sentiments and employments I was so well acquainted with. Pleased and captivated with his person also, I felt inexpressible delight, that I was not indifferent to him; but when I considered the situation we were both in, my sorrow was without bounds. - I spent the night in tears; and my passions, ever impetuous, were a source of misery to me, which found no relief from hope.

The next day, however, I resolved to improve the liberty I had of walking in the same garden, and which I had never an inclination to do before. I went out, and saw the young man at the window, who seemed delighted to see me there; at the next turn I saw him not, but was resolved to take another, in hopes of his returning again; he had retired to write the following billet, which he dropped at my feet. - I looked round, and seeing no one, took it up, and retired with it to my apartment.

An unfortunate man, who has been a prisoner of state more than six years; a stranger to joy; an alien from society, has received from the fair one this is addressed to, a delight unfelt before. Innocent of any crime, yet without any present prospect of a release, let your pity soften my solitude. - Let me have the pleasure of seeing you daily in this garden, and from this let me judge of your compassion.

Courtney.

This note afforded me exquisite delight: I found that this stranger had made an impression on my heart, which nothing could erase.

I waited with impatience the next day for the hour of walking; our eyes met, and easily explained to each other that our love was mutual. From this time, frequent letters to each other imparted our sentiments, while I continued to be the invisible and silent auditor of his solitary amusements: which I was resolved, however, not to inform him of; as I thought it would set him on his guard more, and I should not be enabled to judge so well of the sincerity of his love for me, which I did not doubt would influence his amusements; in this I was not deceived, for instead of learned studies, almost all his attention was now constantly turned to subjects of poetry and sentiment. – Almost every day produced new compositions of his own, on those themes; but the despair which ran through them, awoke my tenderest compassion.

One day, when I was walking in a retired part of the garden, I was surprised to see Courtney hastening to meet me; – as soon as he approached, he said his love and despair had determined him to risk every thing, for the pleasure of a moment's conversation with me; that it was against the rules of the place, for more than one prisoner to be in the garden at once, but that he had got down unobserved by the guard, though he knew he had not a moment to stay. – He then, in lively terms, expressed his passion; entreated me, if ever we were at liberty, to consent to be his; to inform him of my name and abode, and during our captivity, to answer his letters.

My solicitude for his safety, banished all reserve from my words and behaviour; I acknowledged my interest in his safety, and told him, I would inform him by a letter who I was, and any thing else he wished to know, earnestly beseeching him to be gone that instant. He threw himself at my feet, and kissed my hand, in an extacy of gratitude at my condescension, and hastily left me.

The next day I fulfilled my promise, and writ to him, acquainted him with my story, and the little hopes I had of obtaining my liberty; still concealing my knowledge of his solitary employments, but declaring myself so sincerely attached to him, that I did not wish for liberty while he continued a prisoner; recommending it to him, to hope that heaven would not permit us, innocent as we were of any crime against the state, to remain for ever in captivity; and adding, that patience and resignation were the most probable means of lightening, as well as shortening it. I threw this letter out at the window, and saw him take it up.

The next day, I went into the garden as usual, and walked some time, seeing him at the window; he left it, and I withdrew to the retired part of the garden, where I had before seen him, and determined to wait there till he had time to write, which I imagined he had gone away to do, when how was I shocked and surprised, to see him hastening to meet me! knowing, as I did, the danger of it; but I could not persuade him to leave me for nearly half and hour, nor would he permit me to leave him; at length, however, he went away, but he had been observed, and was reprimanded by the keeper severely, though respectfully, and suffered to go into his apartment.

I was soon after returning to mine, but was told, that our connection was discovered; first, by our communication by letters thrown out at the window, and then, by our interview in the garden; that it was an affair by no means to be permitted, and that, therefore, I must retire to another part of the Tower. The keeper then conducted me into the apartment that my poor mother died in, making an apology for his conduct, and saying he must fulfill his orders.

I was so struck with grief and horror at the place I was returned to, that it stopped my utterance, and suspended, at first, every other thought: all the circumstances of my mother's death recurred to my memory, and filled me with the keenest anguish. When I had exhausted those first emotions, I revolved in my mind my distance from Courtney, and the loss, perhaps, for ever, of his society. What a distracting idea! though my feelings were naturally violent, reason and virtue had always some power over them: no reason now came to my aid; even the dictates of religion were unattended to. The passion I felt for Courtney, the despair that the loss of his conversation possessed me with, unsoftened by any friendly remonstrances, undivested by any amusement of avocation, found within my breast a misery too great for any weak frame to support.

A violent fever succeeded the first distraction of my mind; I had every assistance afforded me, and a careful nurse to attend me; but for a long time I was insensible to every thing, and when my body was tolerably restored, a deep melancholy, and perfect indifference to life succeeded. I should not have attended to the food necessary for my existence, had not my nurse used every argument to prevail on me to eat of what they brought, which, to avoid being teized, I did.

At last, I was permitted to walk upon the battlements of the Tower for a little air, but not to go into the garden I used to frequent: my nurse supported my feeble steps, but as I could not walk far, I sat down disconsolately, mourning my hard fate; to be thus removed from the only person in the world who was interested about me, or who felt for me the sweet sentiments of friendship. Yet I, everyday, took the advantage they gave me of quitting my hated cell for a short time, thought a little fresh air was all the benefit I reaped from it, for I neither saw, nor heard, any thing of the unfortunate Courtney. This was my situation on your Majesty's entrance into the Tower, and on your enquiring what prisoners of rank were here, I was brought into your presence.

The fair Laurana here concluded her narrative: the Queen expressed the warmest esteem for her, said she should rejoice to give liberty of person and conscience to all, and to reign over a free people, whom she wished to attach to her, only by her solicitude to render them happy.

She added, that she feared so powerful a Duke as Norfolk, would not be permitted by her council to be set at liberty, and it would be too glaring a partiality to release Courtney without him, till her accession to the crown was a little more ratified by the voice of the people; that Mary was in arms, and the consent doubtful, but that however it terminated, it could not but be favorable to Courtney, and consequently to herself; she therefore entreated her to render herself completely easy, and be assured that they would be permitted to see each other as often as they pleased. She said, she would immediately send again for Courtney, who doubtless was very desirous to entertain his fair mistress.

A messenger was then sent for him, and he soon appeared, with that elegant and noble air, which is the effect of refined sentiments and a great mind. – That sickly languor, which was diffused over his face at his first entrance, was changed to a lively red, at the sight of the fair Lady Laurana.

The Queen, in the most animated terms, expressed her concern, that so amiable a young nobleman should have been so long secluded from society, to which he would have been as ornament. She said, she had frequently regretted his fate, during the life of the late King, as his majesty also had; but he could not prevail on the Protector to release him. She then added the reasons before given to Lady Laurana which obliged her to detain him a little while longer in the Tower; but said, she would contribute all in her power to prevent his feeling himself a prisoner.

Courtney thanked her, with an appearance of ingenuous gratitude, for her goodness to him; and then approaching the object of his tenderest concern, who looked ready to faint, in the most affecting manner, he expressed his joy to see her again, whom he thought he had lost for ever; and a scene to tenderness passed between them, which I can never do justice to; and, indeed, we soon left them, thinking it would be more pleasing to them to enjoy their transports alone.

I afterwards required him to relate what his situation was, when he found he had lost his fair mistress. – He said, he had no intimation given him of Lady Laurana's departure from her room; he therefore watched all the next day for her appearance in the garden, and finding, toward dusk, that she did not come down as usual, he went into it himself, waiting for her appearance at her window, but she appeared not; he then played some of his favorite airs, and sung them to his guitar; still, however, no Laurana appeared, not even for a moment: as the darkest approached, he entreated her, in the most plaintive manner, to give him some signal of her being still in her room; but all in vain, no signal, no answering voice, no Laurana appeared.

Sometimes he thought she was dead; sometimes that she had left the Tower, and that he should never see her again; at other times, his gloomy mind, half-distracted with a horrid suspense, would imagine he heard her voice in screams of agony; he would then start from his bed, and listen with the most fearful attention; when every hollow step, every resounding echo, which broke through the silence of the night, in that mansion of strength, would raise a thousand dreadful ideas, and apparitions of horror to his distempered fancy.

At length time, that soother of grief, a little abated his distraction, and reason assumed, by slow degrees, her power over his soul, which enabled him to have recourse to his studies, and, after a while, allowed him to amuse himself with his guitar.

Though he avoided the subject of love with the greatest industry, he said he one day, without consideration, touched the notes of a little air, with which he first addressed Lady Laurana, on the subject of love. The words recurred to his memory, and, with them, the whole train of those ideas, which had almost deprived him of reason – the effect had almost again deranged his mind, and it was some days before he could recover any thing like tranquility.

This was his situation when the Queen's message reached him: he started from his seat, looked wildly round him, but could not, for a while, comprehend what was meaned by it.

So many events, new and astonishing to a man, who had been a prisoner more than six years, and, in all that time, and never known the least circumstance of what was doing in the world, only that Henry was dead, and succeeded by Edward, a minor, which he had learned from Lady Laurana's story. To be informed, at present, that Edward was also dead; that he had excluded his sister from the succession, and left his Crown to Lady Jane Grey, and that this new Queen had sent for him; what could it mean? to what new fate was he reserved!

Yet he reflected – I may, perhaps, see again my charming Laurana, if she still lives. This hope animated him to appear before the new Queen with some degree of resolution.

Both the Queen and myself were greatly affected, with the sufferings of these amiable lovers, and we shall rejoice exceedingly to see them happy.

Lady Laurana, and myself, are already united in a sincere and tender friendship. I know but of one fault she has, which is a little to much bigotry to the religion she has been brought up in, by which I do not mean constancy, which I approve of as much as she does, but want of charity.

But all her passions and feelings are naturally violent and excessive; yet her manners are gentle, and her heart artless and good, and she takes infinite pains to preserve the authority of reason over her soul. She is a charming woman, and, as her health returns, those beauteous eyes, over which sickness had cast her veil, now shines every day with increasing splendour, as do also her lover's, who is one of the finest figures, and has the most animated countenance I ever saw.

I have written you a long letter, my Catherine. Inform me very soon that your health is amended, which I am exceedingly sorry to hear is so interrupted; and that you will come and pay your duty to your Queen, who has now a claim to your attention superior to that of sister.

Adieu, my dearest cousin,

Your Anne Grey [Lane 114].

Next is Lady Anne's vivid portrait of the dreadful events unfolding in England in a letter to Lady Laurana who was still in a convent in Florence. Lady Laurana's reply tells of her conversion to Protestantism, certainly a large step.

LETTER 27-2

How feelingly, my dear Lady Anne, have you related the past horrid and affecting event! – In what animated forms described your anguish! – And with what sympathy has my heart borne its testimony of sorrow to every tale of woe, as you proceeded! – The circumstances alone are such, indeed, as must excite pity and admiration in every breast not wholly callous.

Blessed martyrs! – Excellent, noble Jane! – I almost envy thy fate! – Happy Lord Guildford too! – United again to thy fair partner: never more to feel the pangs of separation, and the sorrows of absence. United to her in a state, beyond expression blessed.

I am become a convert to thy reformed principles, and abhor persecution, with the other errors of popery, with sincere conviction.

I have a sensible acquaintance here, my dear friend, who is a Protestant; and who has satisfied some of my doubts, in a relation of my mother's, to whom, sister Clara has introduced me, and who has invited me frequently to her house. There I sometimes meet Protestant divines, whose arguments have assisted my conversion.

But what, beyond all this, worked the change, was an English Bible which was lent me; which language, though not my parents, is mine, as I was born in England, and understand it equally with Italian. Almost every chapter in it, strikes conviction into my understanding, and the light of truth into my heart.

My zeal is now so great in favor of my newly acquired faith, that, I think, I should rejoice to be a martyr in its cause. Yet, let me not be too secure; zeal, frequently indiscrete zeal, is the concomitant of new opinions: may mine be moderated by charity, by toleration, by every gentle and humane consideration, which becomes frail and erring creatures to their fellow-beings, be they of what religion they may.

God, who is the author of being, and the former of the human heart, has implanted in every one those sentiments, from climate, constitution, and education, which will best answer the purpose of his providential dispensations. Blest, thrice blest are those, who enjoy the benefit of the Christian revelation! Are enabled to distinguish the light of truth! And enjoy the privileges of such a Gospel! – But those are happy only as their practice conforms with their principles, and who meekly, and with simplicity, receive the precepts of the Gospel, and obey them.

I am rejoiced, my dear Lady Anne, that you have a little recovered your mind from the first shock of your recent misfortunes.

Lady Jane's fortitude, and your resignation, are both the happy effects of your divine principles. – Ah! That I could attain this perfection! – But I must acknowledge, that it is with great difficulty, I can support my too keen apprehensions, concerning the fate of the amiable Earl of Devon. I tremble to open your letters, lest they should contain some dreadful account of his fate.

That impetuous temper, which is natural to me, will not always be controlled; and I am quite ashamed to own, that I am almost distracted by my fears on this account.

I think, I see him condemned by the cruel Mary to horrid tortures! I feel his agonies! And am almost resolved to destroy myself by poison, rather than suffer such acute misery! But, on a sudden, a divine ray from Heaven illuminates my benighted soul! I am feelingly awake to my guilt and danger; supplicate the mercy of the Deity; and again experience that composure, that hope, that resignation, which sincere contrition, is fitted to obtain.

Pity thy poor friend, my dear Lady Anne, and teach me to support, with steadiness, whatever misfortunes are decreed by Heaven to your

Laurana [Lane, Vol. II 128].

History has not recorded the fate of Lady Anne's father John Grey, but both her uncles Henry and Thomas were executed. Lady Anne shielded her fathers' location in France, using only the first letter of the name of his location. The time frame that this next letter represents would have been while Courtenay was out of England, possibly during his period in Italy.

LETTER 28

I was sitting one evening in my solitary apartment, in that kind of composed melancholy, which is cherished by those who have experienced deep afflictions, and which, so far from corroding the heart, softens it to benevolence and compassion, when a servant came to say, that a gentleman wanted to impart something of importance to me, and requested he might speak to me alone; I was surprised at the message, and hesitated, at first, if I had best comply with his request or not; however, I soon admitted him, and how still more surprised and delighted was I, to receive a letter from my father, who writ me, that he had found a safe retreat, at the time that my uncle Suffolk's party was obliged to disperse and hide themselves, and that he remained in it till the search of the Queen's troops was over; that then, by the disguise of a common sailor, he obtained a passage to France, where he then was, and meant to remain, till some happy revolution rendered his country more safe to him.

My father added, that he wanted the consolations of his beloved daughter's company, and was in daily apprehensions for her safety; while she remained in England; he therefore entreated me to commit myself to the care of the gentleman, who was the barer of his letter, and who would convey me safely to him, having a proper disguise, to prevent my being discovered.

Rejoiced as I was, to recover a father whom I had almost given up for lost, my thoughts, from this pleasing circumstance, reverted to my unfortunate friends in the Tower, whom I felt great regret to quit.

I, however, told the gentleman, I was greatly rejoiced to hear of my father's safety, and would prepare myself to attend him in two days. He respectfully urged me to set out immediately, lest it should, by any means, reach the Queen's ears, that my father had sent for me.

I told him, he need be under no apprehension, but that, if possible, I would go sooner: as the Queen had confiscated all the houses and estates of my father, I had been in a friend's house ever since the late troubles; I had therefore very little to take with me, besides some valuable jewels of my mother's and my own.

As soon as my father's messenger was gone, I was preparing myself to visit my friends in the Tower, and to take a final leave of them, which was a task almost too much for my resolution, when, who should I see enter my apartment, but the Earl of Devon.

On hearing his voice, I started from my reveries; yet, like one just awakened from a troublesome dream, could not believe my senses; nor that what I saw was real.

He at last convinced me it was himself, and told me, that the Queen's marriage, which I image you must have heard of, had occasioned his enlargement, from motives which he could not account for, unless it was the wish of popularity; Don Philip had set him at liberty.

We spent two or three hours together, in the painfully-pleasing employment, of conversing on the late melancholy fate of our friends; mixing joy with our tears, that they were now at liberty from Mary's tyranny, their parent's ambition, and all the ills that beset this mortal life.

He, almost at his entrance, asked impatiently if I had heard from you, whom he has so long been utterly excluded from by his confinement, as well as from writing to you.

You will not, I am sure, be angry, if I own I read some parts of your letters to him: he was delighted with them, lamented his hard fate, in being so long separated from you, and said, he was at length permitted to go abroad, as he has obtained the Queen's consent; that he would immediately go to Florence as he was impatient to see you, and as he would make you the offer of his hand; and, if you would consent to marry him, he would reside abroad, till it was more safe for him to reside in his own country.

I entreated him to give me some account of the reasons, that led Mary to suspect him of a passion for Elizabeth, and of their mutually conspiring against her. He said, he would relate the few incidents which had happened to him, since he parted from his dear Lady Laurana, and the unfortunate Lady Jane, at the Tower, which I will give you, as nearly as I can, in his own words.

"When I first came out into the world, and was introduced, by the Queen, to the young nobility at court, I felt so conscious of my want of those accomplishments suited to my rank, and which, the many years I had been immured in prison, had prevented my acquiring, that I was resolved to devote as much of my time as I could to attain them; in the mean time, the Queen's partiality for me, would not suffer me to enjoy so much retirement as I wished for, for that purpose, and which also my long habits of solitary life had rendered almost necessary to me; as well as my love for Lady Laurana, and my earnest desire to form myself, by my address and manners, more worthy of her.

"The reception I met with at Court, however, was too insinuating for a young man, who had been secluded so long from society.

"Not to have many charms, and the only thing that rendered it irksome to me, was my absence from Laurana, and the Queen's passion, which I both dreaded and detested, and which she had very early, after our first acquaintance, got me informed of.

"Her jealously of the Lady Elizabeth, also, who is an amiable Princess, had given me frequent cause of uneasiness; for her conversation, both engaging and instructive to a man like me, who has had so few opportunities of conversing with sensible and well-bred women, had induced me to

196

attach myself a good deal to her, particularly as she showed me great attention.

"The Queen you know hates the Princess, and could not support the idea that I should slight her passion, and devote my time to her sister.

"In vain I assured her, on my honor, that I had never made the slightest effort to gain the Princess's affection.

"She could not believe that I would refuse her hand and crown, without the prospect of an equivalent at some future period.

"I entreated her Majesty to permit me to go abroad; expressed my earnest desire to see foreign courts, and to get a knowledge of the customs and manners of other nations, but she would by no means consent to it.

"As I generally informed Elizabeth of the Queen's threats concerning her, she thought it best to retire from court into the country, as she met with every instance of disrespect, that the Queen could show her in public.

"And not long after Wyatt's insurrection (which has been so fatal to the Duke of Suffolk's family) commenced, Elizabeth and myself were accused of being concerned in it, and both committed to different prisons.

"But as Wyatt, on his execution, entirely acquitted us of having the least concern in it, the Lady Elizabeth was tried by the Council, and vindicated her innocence so well, that the Queen was obliged to release her from confinement, as well as myself; at that time, more from the fear of the people than inclination.

"For she soon found another pretence of confiding her again, which was by proposing an alliance for her with the Duke of Savoy; which, however, that Princess, in a submissive manner, begged leave to decline, saying, she wished to remain single. But this was construed into a confirmation of an engagement with me; and, in the resistance she made to her Majesty's pleasure, she found as she thought, a sufficient plea to confine her to Woodstock, and to send me to Fotheringay Castle.

"Here we remained till the Queen's marriage with Don Philip, and his affection for popularity induced him to release those of the Nobility which Mary had confined on suspicion, amongst the rest myself, and also to undertake the defense of the Princess Elizabeth from the malice of her sister.

"He, therefore, sat her at liberty, much to the disgust of the Queen, who, I believe, already perceives that Philip is more influenced by ambitious views than love to her.

"The Princess has not, however, since been at Court, but I received a message from her, soon after our enlargement, requesting to speak with me.

"I immediately visited her, and we met with expressions of that friendship, which a similarity of sentiments and dispositions had united us in.

"She told me, she had continually regretted that the Queen's unjust suspicions of me, on her account, should have been so injurious to me; and that she would willingly undertake any thing that might contribute to my happiness, and should rejoice to make any compensation for my past sufferings on her account. She said, there was something in my manner at times, which convinced her that some Lady had possession of my affections, though I dare not own it, on account of the Queen's partiality for me; but now her Majesty was married, she thought she had influence enough with Philip to engage him to promote the alliance; she, therefore besought me to consider her as my sincere friend, and to unfold to her my inclinations without reserve.

"I was struck with her goodness, but yet was at a loss what to do. Elizabeth, though possessed of eminent virtues, is vain, and fond of admiration.

"I had, on many occasions, observed, that she did not like that any Lady should have the preference to herself, not only in mine, but in the opinion of those Lords about her, whom she favored with any marks of attention.

"I thought too, that there was something in her manner confused, and as if she meant, by an appearance of generosity, to draw me into a declaration of particular attachment to herself; and if so, instead of extricating myself from the difficulties that lay in my way to the possession of Laurana, by my confidence in the Princess, I should only, perhaps, be involving myself in greater.

"What could I do? I had not seen enough of courts, and the deceits of them, to submit to the meanness of a lie. I was silent and confused; it was some time, before I could recollect myself sufficiently to thank her, for the interest she took in my happiness; to beg she would not urge me on a subject which I must ever be silent on, and to assure her, that the sense of her goodness would never be erased from my heart; and that, wherever my fate drove me, the Princess Elizabeth would ever possess the most sincere friendship of Devonshire.

"The Princess blushed, and I perceived that this speech flattered her vanity; she evidently imputed my confusion and reserve, to a passion for herself, which my respect for her, and the situation we were in, forbade my revealing.

"I was rejoiced, therefore, that I had not revealed my secret; and she did not urge me any more on the subject, but desired me to inform her if, in any thing, she could be serviceable to me with Don Philip.

"I told her, I thought myself very insecure in England, in my present situation, and had also a wish to improve myself by travel, and, if she would have the goodness to desire Don Philip to intercede with the Queen for that purpose, I should esteem myself infinitely obliged to her, though I should still regret the loss of her conversation, which had afforded me so many agreeable hours.

"The Princess took my compliment graciously, and promised to endeavor to obtain my desire, which she soon after effected.

"I went to court, to thank the Queen for this permission, but she would not see me, which I was no otherwise concerned at, than as it may affect the Princess's safety. I have seen Lady Elizabeth several times since, who has always shown me great attention, and friendly solicitude for my welfare.

"I am ready now to set out, and will, with pleasure, convey whatever letters, or message, you may have to your friend, my charming Laurana: the impatience which I suffer to behold her again cannot be equaled."

I informed the Earl, when he had ended his account, that my father was in safety, in France, and desired me to join him there; that he had sent a messenger to convey me to him, and that I should set out in two days.

He seemed quite rejoiced at the event; he said he would prepare himself to accompany me, and that when he had obtained his Laurana's hand, he would endeavor to prevail on her, to make mine the place of their residence.

Then, added he, I may hope for an amiable female companion for my wife, which will contribute to her happiness, and with still so many worthy friends about us, may I not flatter myself that, in spite of the past cruelty of my fate, I shall be one of the happiest of mortals?

I objected to his accompanying me as highly improper, since it would lay open my father's situation, and our affairs to the inspection of the Queen, in all probability; that he would go abroad in a manner suitable to his rank, but that I had a disguise provided for me, and should go in the most private manner that was possible.

He said, he could not prevail on himself to permit me to go, attended only by a stranger; that therefore, if I would pardon him, he would recommend to me to go in disguise, and attended by this gentleman, in his train, or, as passengers in the same vessel; that as soon as they were landed on the French shore, he would privately attend me, and commit me in safety to my father's arms.

I thanked him very sincerely, and said, I had no objection to his proposal, but the apprehension, least he should render himself liable to the Queen's displeasure, should we be discovered; or that, my father's asylum being found out, the consequences might be fatal to him; and those fears, I owned, were so great, that I should not enjoy a moment's peace during my voyage. I therefore declined his offer, and determined in the disguise prepared for me, and under the protection of the gentleman my father had sent, to commit myself to Providence, and take my voyage.

I went and took a sorrowful leave of my friends in the Tower, who expressed a great and generous pleasure in my father's safety, notwithstanding their own sad fate, and prayed that I might safely join my father.

They also found pleasure in the Earl's release, and prospect of happiness, and discovered those great and worthy minds, which, though under the chastening hand of Heaven themselves, can rejoice without envy at the felicity of their friends and fellow creatures.

Long we lingered before we could think of parting, and nothing but the approach of night could tear me from them; and, even then, I thought, was I to consult my own inclination, I had rather, at the time, have remained with them to console and entertain them, than forsake them in so bitter a fate. – But my father's will, and his want of an affectionate daughter, to render his exile more tolerable, enabled me to make a violent effort of resolution, and quit the place.

But adieu – perhaps forever! I could not say!

No sleep scarcely had I that night, but wept almost incessantly.

My father's messenger appeared in the morning, and brought with him my disguise – I told him I should be ready to attend him in the evening, and desired him to prepare every thing for me, and return early.

I had taken leave of my friend, in whose house I was, and was preparing to depart, when I was surprised by the appearance of the Earl, completely disguised as well as myself; who said he could not suffer me to set out without his protection; that, therefore, he had given orders that his suit should go in the vessel they were designed for, and told them and the captain, that he was obliged himself to sail in another ship.

Though much alarmed for his safety, he would hear none of my objections, and we went on board of the vessel provided for me.

As soon as we had sat down in the cabin, the Earl entered into an agreeable conversation, which a little dissipated my melancholy thoughts at quitting England, perhaps for ever, that recent scene of so much bloodshed, and so many horrors; but it was the recollection of my unhappy friends, that rendered my heart heavy; nor could I banish them from my idea, for in spite of his endeavors to awaken more pleasing and cheerful remembrances, our conversation adverted to them.

Yet, he still encouraged me to hope, that they would soon be released; that it would be of no consequence to the Queen to keep them confined, since their party was quelled entirely. He entreated me, therefore, to endeavor to banish sorrow from my heart, and to sympathize with him in his extreme joy, at the thoughts of seeing again his charming Lady Laurana.

I told him, I would endeavor to do it, in the hopes he had given me, that my captive friends would soon be at liberty. I began to look forward also, as the shore of France approached, to the pleasure of seeing again a father, for whom I had the sincerest duty and affection, preserved from the wreck of fate. I felt the most affecting gratitude to Heaven, for this consolation in my heavy afflictions; and for that goodness, which had not suffered me to sink under them, but preserved me to assist in supporting and comforting my exiled father.

Thus, I am persuaded, will all those, who listen to the divine lessons of resignation in their sorrows, have reason for gratitude in the midst of the severest fate; even though they cannot penetrate the veil of Providence, nor understand why they are thus severely dealt with.

I had began this letter before I received yours, which both delighted and shocked me. I was charmed to think that you had abjured the errors of popery; admired your sentiments on zeal and charity; but how was I shocked at the account of your impatience at the confinement of the Earl! – May Heaven preserve the reason of my friend, exclaimed I, with fervor! – O! may she be preserved from destroying herself! – from abruptly presenting a guilty soul, stained with suicide, before a pure and righteous God! – O! lay not on her more than her frail nature can support!

I congratulate you, my fair friend, on the happiness that awaits you. – Write to me at B-, where my father is. – I send this from the first inn we put up at in France. We remain here to-night, and in the morning, proceed on our journey to B-.

The Earl is resolved to accompany me; my father will rejoice to see him: his own ship and suite are not yet arrived; he has only one servant with him, in whom he can confide. – My father intends to meet me half way. With what delight shall I see him again, after so long an absence?

Farewell, my charming Laurana; you have with this a letter from the Earl.

Anne Grey [Lane 136].

The next letter is a short continuation of the previous letter.

LETTER 29

I found my father at the place he appointed to meet me, in perfect health. He received me with every testimony of extreme joy – yet a moment after, it was suddenly checked by the bitter recollection of all we and our friends had suffered since our separation. We offered the tribute of a few tears to the memory of the martyred pair.

When my father, resuming his composure, expressed again his joy at seeing me, and declared, that in respect to his own share in the late calamities, he had already forgot all his past sorrows in his present happiness.

Judge, my dear Laurana, what pleasure I received from this information, and if I was not again reconciled to life – since I was become of so much consequence to the felicity of the best of parents.

The Earl partook of my joy, as my father did in his approaching happiness, and we retired to our apartments with those pleasing impressions on our hearts, which usually procure sweet and sound repose.

We cannot prevail with the Earl to remain more than one day with us – to-morrow he sets out, and with him this letter, which, therefore, I have not time to lengthen.

May no ill accident impede his speedy arrival at Florence, and may all happiness attend him and my fair friend, prays her

Anne Grey [Lane, Vol. II 172].

The time that the following letter appears to represent is late May or early June of 1555 after Courtenay's release from the Tower and departure from England. Laurana wrote Lady Anne informing her of their marriage to Courtenay.

LETTER 30

With greater joy than I can express, I beheld again my amiable Devonshire, improved in person and manners, and blest with a heart noble, generous, and sincere; such a heart as Queens have been proud to have called their own.

About a month after his arrival we were married; but how unworthy do I esteem myself of such a treasure?

I have informed him of the change you were the first means of causing in my religious sentiments. His opinion very nearly coincide with mine, and our happiness is more complete on this account; indeed it is impossible for any woman to possess a more tender and affectionate husband, and I only wish for the presence of my dear Lady Anne to crown my felicity, and to see her united to a man equally amiable with the Earl of Devon.

Flatter me with the hopes of your company before the year is at an end, and be assured that my own happiness has not rendered me selfish, but that I have a heart, as open to all the feelings of friendly sympathy as ever.

I was charmed at the account the Earl gave me of your interview with your father; how happy am I that you are safe under his protection, and out of the reach of the resentful Mary. But shall I own, that I sometimes have apprehensions invade my mind, lest her malice should snatch my husband from me.

No one knows the secret of our marriage, but the relation of my mother's, whom I mentioned, and at whose house I live, whose disposition is too amiable to doubt her fidelity; sister Clara, whom I parted from with regret, and our two confidential servants.

The Earl has a house of his own, where his servants are, but you may imagine, the greatest part of his time he passes with me; thus has he guarded against a discovery: but the uncertainty of all earthly happiness, cannot but check our transports, and ought not allow of too great an elation of mind, which is inconsistent with our state of trial, and would attach us too much to the world, and draw us off from our pursuit of a better.

The Earl joins with me in every good wish to your father and yourself.

Adieu.

Laurana [Lane 176].

In the next and final of the "Lane letters", Lady Laurana indicates to Lady Anne in the second paragraph, why history has not recorded her marriage to Edward Courtenay.

LETTER 32

With pleasure, my dear Lady Anne, we comply with your father's and your request, and are preparing to visit you very soon; the Earl only waits for letters from England: he means to take no English servant with him, besides the one whom he confides in; and I shall only have my woman, who is acquainted with our marriage.

We propose taking a house near your's, and remaining as long as circumstances of conveniency will admit. We mean to conceal our real names and quality, and to hire servants from the place you are at. This, I think, must elude Mary's vigilance; for, I assure you, we are liable to discovery here, from Mary's religion, and acquaintance with priests and cardinals: many of those residing here, the Earl knows, and as he has lately been rendered a conspicuous character, from the Queen's attention to him, these priests are too busy a set of beings, and too desirous to ingratiate themselves with her, not to give her so important a piece of information, as his marriage without her knowledge and consent. On the whole, therefore, it will be best for us to quit Florence on every account; though I regret leaving sister Clara, and the good Lady with whom I live, and considers me as her child.

We shall not wait for your reply, but set out as soon as possible. – You cannot imagine the pleasure I receive at the prospect of seeing you again, after so long an absence.

I rejoice that the Duchess of Suffolk is at liberty; God grant that Lady Catherine may be restored to her health.

Adieu, my dear friend, may our interview be a happy one.

Laurana [Lane, Vol. II 188].

Admittedly, the letters are of questionable authenticity and cannot be relied upon as an accounting of facts. However, even if they are fictional, and the creation of a skilled writer, presumably having an agenda of his or her own, at the very least they appear to be based upon personal knowledge or researched material, as many of the events mentioned in the letters did actually occur and they give a modern reader some sense of the flavor of the times.

Chapter 8. Furthermore

As with most research projects that set out to answer questions, more questions often result from those answered, and this chapter will cover some of those issues.

Missing Letters

An intriguing question is the fate of certain letters that Courtenay left behind after he died. There is a short trail that began on 17 November 1556, in which the Council of Ten in Venice had instructed the bailiff of Padua to wrap the casket (box) containing Courtenay's writings in a wrapping that would hide the contents for transportation, and to perform this task cautiously and secretly without informing or discussing it with anyone.

Three days later the Council of Ten voted unanimously on a motion to hire a carpenter that possessed certain qualifications and swear him to silence. They would open the sealed casket (box) and review all the letters inside, and then the carpenter would return the casket to the state it was in before it was opened.

By 26 November, all of the letters contained in the casket were reviewed, and the Council of Ten placed a small cross on each of the letters they reviewed. Some were returned to their bundles and others returned to their linen covers, stitched closed, and placed back in the casket as they were first found as to make them appear that they were undisturbed. Then the casket was closed and sealed in the presence of the retinue of Courtenay and sealed with his official seal.

Rawdon Brown, editor of the *Calendar of State Papers and Manuscripts. Relating to English Affairs Existing in the Archives and Collections of Venice* indicated that, of the thirty-two drafts of letters to and from Courtenay he reviewed, which at the time were preserved in the Venetian archives dating 8 May 1555 to 22 February 1556, not one of those letters contained a cross.

Based on that evidence, it would be safe to speculate that the letters were of either some personal or political importance, possibly correspondence to or from the French King expressing a desire to place Courtenay of the throne.

Perhaps the Council of Ten had seized the letters by the request of the Bishop of Lodeve, then the French Ambassador in Venice. There appears to be no reason why the Republic of Venice would commit an act of state larceny by opening a sealed container, as they had no reason to be curious about the letters; but the French certainly would.

In what is the last known reference to such letters, on 21 June 1557, Doctor Wotton wrote to Queen Mary mentioning an interview with a gentleman named Lant, who had some ties with the French, and who had told a correspondent of Doctor Wotton's that he had in his possession certain letters that once belonged to Courtenay. When he was later questioned about them, he denied that he had ever said such a thing or had ever been in possession of letters of the late Courtenay.

There are no further indications or suggestions as to where any of the letters went, who received them, how many there actually were, or additional information as to their whereabouts or disposition of the letters marked by the Council. They were most likely destroyed, forever concealing their contents, not only to possibly protect Courtenay's name, but anyone who was mentioned in the letters and their intrigues. Perhaps some of these letters lie in an obscure collection of manuscripts somewhere that have yet to be discovered. Any correlation with the Lane letters?

WYATT'S REBELLION

The question of Courtenay's involvement in Thomas Wyatt's rebellion is yet another intrigue that most likely was hidden by several skillful consorts close to Courtenay.

Setting aside the unsubstantiated claims that many historians have made regarding Courtenay's involvement in Wyatt's rebellion, one early historian makes a point on which I agree: after having spent slightly half of his life imprisoned in the Tower, it would be safe to speculate that Courtenay would have enjoyed his new freedom, and it seems very unlikely that he would have done anything to jeopardize it, especially by committing an act of treason, which joining or leading a rebellion against the Queen would be, and would most certainly have resulted in his execution.

Further evidence to support Courtenay's lack of involvement could be the thorough investigation that would have resulted from Thomas Wyatt's accusation upon his capture of Courtenay and Elizabeth's involvement. History has recorded no ill results of any findings, and the fact that Courtenay was eventually released from the Tower with his head still on his shoulders could in part lend some credence to his innocence.

It was revealed during the trial of Nicholas Throckmorton, which occurred on 17 April 1554, just after Thomas Wyatt was executed, that Throckmorton was to ride with Courtenay and join Peter Carew and raise the counties of Devon and Cornwall. Several confessions had been read that also placed Courtenay in locations that could have given him the opportunity to conspire with Wyatt during the formation of the plans for the rebellion.

Quite probably, Courtenay may have known about Wyatt and Carew's plans, and in the very beginning may have given some indication that he was in agreement with them, as history has recorded the fact that he was displeased with Mary's choice for a husband and had even told her so. Realizing the severity of the situation, Courtenay may have been influenced by someone close to him, such as the Chancellor, and withdrawn before any real damage to his integrity was done. Some evidence remains that the Chancellor may have purposely omitted Courtenay's name from some documents that could have been detrimental to his survival.

ILLNESS OR POISON

As with many from this turbulent period of history, the possibility of death by murder or poison could, and sometimes does, exist, and one could easily point to signs that could be interpreted to suggest the same fate for Edward Courtenay.

In early June of 1555, Courtenay was introduced to Frederico Badoer, who later wrote about his meeting with Courtenay in cipher, "that he (Courtenay) was evidently in great fear for his life, and thought of nothing but preserving it; though he had no suspicion of the Emperor, whose audience of him had been loving."

In August 1555, a Spaniard killed a servant of Courtenay's while they were in Brussels. On two separate earlier occasions, Courtenay and his attendants had quarrels with Spaniards and the Spaniards had pursued them to their lodgings.

In September 1555, Courtenay's attendants were again attacked in relation, it was believed, to some earlier dispute. Four of his attendants were wounded, as well as several of the Spaniards. Courtenay informed the Bishop of Arras that there had been four assaults on himself and his attendants.

Perhaps responding to the previous threats and wishing to prevent any further attacks, shortly after his arrival in Venice Courtenay requested a license to carry weapons for himself and twenty-five of his attendants, which the Council of Ten granted.

On 13 July 1556, shortly before Courtenay's death, Doctor Wotton had written to Sir William Petre quoting what the Abbot of St. Saluces had said to the Emperor's Ambassador, "I ween [think] we shall lose the Earl of Devon." Unfortunately, there are no other references or information beyond that statement that could indicate what the Abbot had in mind. Perhaps it was a reference to Courtenay's illness.

On 22 September of the same year, Francisco de Vargas wrote to the Princess Dowager of Portugal and informed her of Courtenay's death. "Courtenay died in this city four days ago of a fever, which carried him off in fourteen days. Everyone was sorry about this, but with his death his intrigues will cease and there will be less trouble in England, now that this inducement had been removed."

The missing letters mentioned earlier may have shed more light on the intrigues that Courtenay was involved in or planning. There is only one known account of the incident that

Courtenay had become ill, as reported by Vannes when Courtenay was at Lio, and it is the one that history has recorded as the true cause of Courtenay's death.

OTHER WORKS RELATING TO EDWARD COURTENAY

While researching material, I encountered two plays; one titled *Courtenay, Earl of Devon; or the Troubles of the Princess Elizabeth, A tragedy*, that was published in 1706, and the second, *The famous history of Sir Thomas Wyatt, with the coronation of Queen Mary*, published in London, 1607. Though neither of these works is of any significant historical value, they do include events from the period when Mary was first crowned and references to the (alleged) secret affair of Elizabeth and Courtenay.

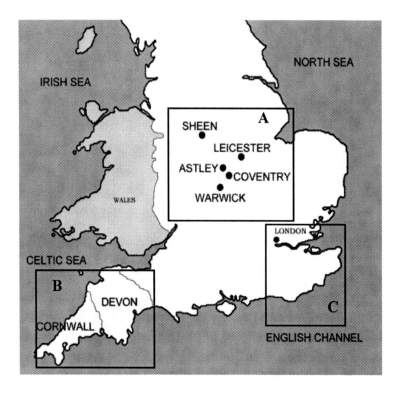

[NOT TO SCALE]

MAP 1. Wyatt's proclamations against the Queen were issued in three main areas.

The proclamatinos were issued by:

A. The Duke of Suffolk in the North;

B. Peter Carew in the counties of Devon and Cornwall (Courtenay was to lead these counties);

C. Thomas Wyatt in Kent and London.

[NOT TO SCALE]

MAP 2. Towns where Wyatt's proclamations were made.

BIBLIOGRAPHY

PRIMARY SOURCES

Aikin, Lucy. *Memoirs of The Court of Queen Elizabeth*. In two volumes. Longman, Hurst, Rees, Orme and Brown. Paternoster Row London, 1818.

—— *Calendar of State Papers and Manuscripts. Relating to English Affairs, Existing in the Archives and collections of Venice*. Vol. V. 1534-1554, Rawdon Brown, Longman & Co. 1873. Vol. VI Part I 1555-1556, Rawdon Brown, Longman & Co. London 1877. Vol. VI Part II 1556-1557, Rawdon Brown, Longman & Co. London 1881.

Cleaveland, E. *A Genealogical History of the Noble and Illustrious Family of Courtenay*. Exon: printed by Edward Farley at Shakespear's Head. 1735.

Chapman, Hester W. *Lady Jane Grey – The Nine Day Queen*. London England: Jonathan Cape, 30 Bedford Square, 1962.

——*The Last Tudor King. A Study of Edward VI*. London England: Jonathan Cape, thirty Bedford Square, 1958.

Collins, Arthur. *Letters and Memorials of State, in the Reigns of Queen Mary, Queen Elizabeth, King James*. London, England: T. Osborne, 1746.

Courtenay, Edward. *The Benefit of Christ's Death, an English version made in 1548*. Bell & Daldy. London, 1855.

England, Proclamation, Chronological series. This is a collection of the proclamations issued during the reigns of Edward VI, Lady Jane, and Mary I. Printed by John Cawodi, London, 1553-1554.

Heylyn, Peter. *Ecclesia Restaurata, or The History of the Reformation of the Church of England. An Appendex to the former book touching the Interposings made in Behalf of the Lady Jane Gray.* London England: H. Twyford, 1661.

Lindsay, Philip. *The Queenmaker, A Portrait of John Dudley.* London England: Williams and Norgate LTD., 1951.

Nichols, John Gough, Esq. *The Chronicle of Queen Jane and of Two Years of Queen Mary and Especially of the Rebellion of Sir Thomas Wyat.* London England: AMS Press, 1850.

Robinson, Rev. Hastings. *Original Letters Relative to the English Reformation, written during the Reigns of King Henry VIII, King Edward VI, and Queen Mary.* New York: Johnson Reprint Corp., 1846.

Strype, John. *Historical Memorials, Ecclesiastical and Civil, of Events under the Reign of Queen Mary I.* Volume III. London. Printed by S. Richardson for John Wyat. 1721.

—— *Ecclesiastical Memorials; Relating chiefly to Religion and the Reformation of it.* Printed for J. Osborn, London 1733. *Volume I, Henry VIII. Volume II, Edward VI. Volume III, Mary I.*

Tytler, Patrick Fraser. *England under the reigns of Edward VI and Mary, with the contemporary history of Europe.* Richard Bentley, London 1839.

SECONDARY SOURCES

Abridgement of the History of England. Being a Summary of Mr. Rapin's History and Mr. Tindal's Continuation. Printed for John Paul Knapton, London 1747.

Adventures and Amours of the Marquis de Noailles and Mademoiselle Tencin. Printed in Ludgate Street, London 1746.

Baumgartner, Frederic. *Henry II, King of France 1547-1559.* Duke University Press, 1988.

Beer, Barrett L. *Rebellion and Riot.* Kent Ohio: The Kent State University Press, 1982.

Blakey, Dorothy. *The Minerva Press 1790-1820.* London, England: University Press, Oxford, 1939.

Biographia Britannica, of the Lives of the Most Eminent Persons who have Florished in Great Britain. Rivington and Marshall, London 1789.

Brown, D. (printed for.) *The History of the Life, Bloody Reign and Death of Queen Mary, Eldest Daughter of Henry VIII.* London 1682.

Burnet, Gilbert. *The History of the Reformation of the Church of England.* T.H, London 1679.

Byrne, M. St. Clare. *The Letters of King Henry VIII.* London England: Cassell and Co. LTD., 1936.

Carte, Thomas. *A General History of England.* 4 Volumes. London England, 1752.

Calendar of the Carew Manuscripts, Preserved in the Archiepiscopal Library at Lambeth 1515-1574. Longmans, Green, Reader & Dyer, London 1867.

Calendar of Letters, Despatches, and State Papers relating to the negotiations between England the Spain. Royall Tyler. Longman, Green, Longman & Roberts.

    Volume X Edward VI 1550-1552 London 1932.

    Volume XI Edward VI and Mary, 1553 London, 1916.

    Volume XII Mary January-July, 1554 London 1949.

    Volume XIII Philip and Mary, July 1554-November 1558 London 1954.

Calendar of the Patent Rolls. Philip and Mary.

    Volume I, 1553-1554 Kraus-Thomson. Nendeln/Liechtenstein, 1970.

    Volume III, 1555-1557, London 1938

    Volume IV, 1557-1558

Calendar of State Papers, Domestic Series, of the reigns of Edward VI., Mary, Elizabeth, 1547-1580. Edited by Lemon, Robert. Longman, Brown, Green, Longmans & Roberts. London 1856.

Calendar of State Papers and Manuscripts. Domestic Series. Of the Reign of Elizabeth 1601-1603 with addenda, 1547-1565. Edited by Green, Mary Anne Everett. Longman & Co. London, 1870.

Calendar of State Papers. Foreign Series. Of the Reign of Mary, 1553-1558. Longman, Green, Longman & Roberts. London 1861.

Calendar of State Papers and Manuscripts, Milan. The Hereford Times Limited, London 1912.

Cecill, William. *A Collection of State Papers relating to affairs in the reigns of King Henry VIII, King Edward VI, Queen Mary, Queen Elizabeth.* Lord Burghley London, 1760.

Clapman, John, *Elizabeth of England.* University of Pennsylvania Press, Philadelphia, Pennsylvania. 1951.

Christopherson, John. *An Exhortation to all Menne to take hede of rebellion.* London, July 1554.

Complete History of England; with the Lives of all the Kings and Queens. London 1706.

Collins, Arthur. *Letters and Memorials of State, in the Reigns of Queen Mary, Queen Elizabeth, King James....* London England: T. Osborne, 1746.

Copland, W. *The Copie of the publication of the trewse made between the most Cristien Kyne Henry Second.* London 1555 or 1556.

Cox, Nicholas. *Courtnay Earl of Devon; or, the Troubles of the Princess Elizabeth, a Tragedy.* London, 1707.

Creighton, Mandell Rev. *The Age of Elizabeth.* Longmans, Green and Co. London, 1899.

Days, John. *The Second Volume of the Ecclesiasticall History, conteynyng the Actes and Monumentes of Martyrs.* London, 1570.

Ellis, Henry. *Original Letters relative to the English Reformation.* London England: R. Bentley, 3 series, 1825, 1827 and 1846.

Erickson, Carolly. *The First Elizabeth* Summit Books, New York, New York. 1983.

Godwin, Francis. *Annals of England: Containing the Reigns of Henry the Eighth, Edward the Sixth, Queen Mary.* London England: by W.G. for T. Basset, 1675.

Godwyn, Morgan. *Annals of England Containing the Reigns of Henry VIII, Edward VI and Queen Mary.* Printed by W.G. 1675.

Harbison, Harris. *Rival Ambassadors at the Court of Queen Mary.* Princeton University Press, London 1940.

Harley, Robert, Earl of Oxford. *Catalogue of the Harleian Collection of Manuscripts in the British Museum.* London England: by D. Leach, 1759 edition

Heylyn, Peter. *Exam Historicum, or, a Discovery and examination of the Mistakes, Falsities and Defects in some Modern Historics.* London, 1659.

—— *Ecclesia Restaurata, or The History of the Reformation of the Church of England. An Appendex to the former book touching the Interposings made in Behalf of the Lady Jane Gray.* London England: H. Twyford, 1661.

Holinshed, Raphael. *The First and Second Volumes of Chronicles, Comprising the Description and History of England, Ireland and Scotland.* London: Henry Denham, 1587.

Holt, Mack P. *Renaissance and Reformation France, 1500-1648.* Oxford University Press, 2002.

Howes, Edmund. *Annales, or A Generall Chronicle of England.* London, 1631.

—— *Impartial Account of Richard Duke of York's Treasons.* Printed for Allen Banks, London, 1671.

Hume, David, Esq. *The History of England.* In 6 volumes. London England for A. Miller, 1762.

Innes, Arthur D. *England under the Tudors.* G.P Putman's Sons. New York 1905.

Kidgell, John, *An Abridgement of Sr. Richard Bakers Chronicle of the Kings of England.* London England: John Kidgell, 1684

Loades, David. *Two Tudor Conspiracies.* Page Brothers, Norwich 1992.

—— *Mary Tudor, A Life.* Basil Blackwell, Oxford 1989.

—— *John Dudley, Duke of Northumberland 1504-1553.* Oxford England: Clarendon Press, 1996.

Loach, Jennifer. *Edward VI.* New Haven Connecticut: Yale University Press, 1999.

Lodge, Edmund, Esq. *Illustrations of British History, Biography, and Manners, in the Reigns of Henry VIII, Edward VI, Mary, Elizabeth, and James I.* London: J. Chidley, 1838.

Loftie, W.J. *Authorised Guide to the Tower of London.* London: for H.M. Stationary Office by Harrison & Son, 1908.

Longford, Elizabeth. *The Oxford Book of Royal Anecdotes.* Oxford University Press, 1991.

Love, Ronald. *Blood and Religion: the conscience of Henry IV, 1553-1593.* McGill-Queen's University Press, 2001.

Luke, Mary. *A Crown for Elizabeth.* Coward-McCann, Inc. New York, 1970.

Kempe, Alfred John, Esq. *The Loseley Manuscripts.* London England by J. Murry, 1836.

King, J. *A Breviat Chronicle: containing al the kynes, from Brute to this daye.* 1554.

Maclean, John Esq. *The Life and Times of Sir Peter Carew, Kt.* Bell and Daldy, London 1857.

Malfatti, C.V. *The Accession Coronation and Marriage of Mary Tudor.* Barcelona, 1956.

Neale, J.E. *Elizabeth I and Her Parliaments 1559-1581.* Jonathan Cape, Thirty Bedford Square, London.

Nichols, John Gough. *The Diary of Henry Machyn, Citizen and Merchant Taylor of London from A.D. 1550 to A.D. 1563.* London 1848.

Nicolas, Nicholas Harris. *The Literary Remains of Lady Jane Grey.* Harding, Triphook and Lepard. London 1825.

Norfolk Archaeology: or Miscellaneous tracts relating to the Antiquities of the County of Norfolk. Published by the Norfolk and Norwich Archaeology Society. Norwich, 1855.

Pollard, A.F. *Tudor Tracts, 1532-1588.* Archibald Constable and Co., LTD. Westminster 1903.

Potter, David. *A History of France, 1460-1560.* Basingstoke, Hampshire England, Macmillan, 1995.

Prescott, H.F.M. *Mary Tudor.* The Macmillan Company, New York 1953.

Proctor, John. *The History of Wyates Rebellion.* London, 1554.

Rapin de Thoyras (Paul). *An Abridgement of the History of England. Being a summary of Mr. Rapin's History.* John and Paul Knapton, London 1747.

Roelker, Nancy Lyman. *One King, One Faith: The parlement of Paris and the religious reformation of the sixteenth century.* Berkley, University of California Press, 1996.

Sanford, Francis. *A Genealogical History of the Kings of England and Monarchs of Great Britain.* Thomas Newcomb. London 1677.

Scarisbrick, J. J. *Henry VIII.* University of California Press, 1968.

Scott, Ronald McNair. *Robert the Bruce, King of Scots.* Peter Bedrick Books, New York 1982.

Strype, John. *Memorials of the Most Reverend Father in God, Thomas Cranmer, sometime Lord Archbishop of Canterbury.* In three books. London: R. Chiswell, 1694.

Taylor, I.A. *Lady Jane Grey and Her Times.* London England: Huchinson & Co., 1908.

Tittler, Robert. *The Reign of Mary I.* Longman Group Limited, 1983.

Waley, John. *A Table collected of the yeres of our lord God, and of the yeres of the Kings of England.* London, 1567.

INDEX

Printed in the United States
65197LVS00002B/109

9 780875 864730